The Panizzi Lectures
1999

Previously published Panizzi Lectures

BIBLIOGRAPHY AND THE SOCIOLOGY OF TEXTS
    by D. F. McKenzie (*1985*)

ENGLISH MONARCHS AND THEIR BOOKS
    by T. A. Birrell (*1986*)

A NATIONAL LIBRARY IN THEORY AND IN PRACTICE
    by K. W. Humphreys (*1987*)

DAPHNIS AND CHLOE:
THE MARKETS AND METAMORPHOSES OF AN UNKNOWN BESTSELLER
    by Giles Barber (*1988*)

THE DUTCH AND THEIR BOOKS IN THE MANUSCRIPT AGE
    by J. P. Gumbert (*1989*)

ERASMUS, COLET AND MORE:
THE EARLY TUDOR HUMANISTS AND THEIR BOOKS
    by J. B. Trapp (*1990*)

THE ENGLISH BOOK IN EIGHTEENTH-CENTURY GERMANY
    by Bernhard Fabian (*1991*)

HEBREW MANUSCRIPTS OF EAST AND WEST:
TOWARDS A COMPARATIVE CODICOLOGY
    by Malachi Beit-Arié (*1992*)

THE MANUSCRIPT LIBRARY OF SIR ROBERT COTTON
    by Colin Tite (*1993*)

MUSIC, PRINT AND CULTURE IN EARLY SIXTEENTH-CENTURY ITALY
    by Iain Fenlon (*1994*)

MAPS AS PRINTS IN THE ITALIAN RENAISSANCE
    by David Woodward (*1995*)

THE INTRODUCTION OF ARABIC LEARNING INTO ENGLAND
    by Charles Burnett (*1996*)

THE HISTORY OF BOOKBINDING AS A MIRROR OF SOCIETY
    by Mirjam M. Foot (*1997*)

PUBLISHING DRAMA IN EARLY MODERN EUROPE
    by Roger Chartier (*1998*)

The Panizzi Lectures
1999

Lost Books of Medieval China

GLEN DUDBRIDGE

THE BRITISH LIBRARY

© 2000 Glen Dudbridge

First published 2000 by
The British Library
96 Euston Road
St Pancras
London NW1 2DB

Cataloguing in Publication Data
A catalogue record for this title is
available from The British Library

ISBN 0 7123 4688 0

Designed by John Mitchell
Typeset by Bexhill Phototypesetters, Bexhill-on-Sea
Printed in Great Britain by Henry Ling Ltd., at the Dorset Press,
Dorchester, Dorset.

Contents

Lecture I
Documenting the Loss   1

Lecture II
Reconstruction: the case of
Summary documents of three kingdoms   27

Lecture III
Classification: the case of
The Four Gentlemen of Liang   53

Lost Books of Medieval China

Chronology

Qin	221–206 BC
Han	206 BC–AD 220
Three Kingdoms	AD 221–280
Southern dynasties	265–589
Liang	502–557
Emperor Wu	502–549
Emperor Yuan	552–555
Chen	557–589
Northern dynasties	386–581
Northern Wei	386–534
Western Wei / Eastern Wei	535–556 / 534–550
Northern Zhou / Northern Qi	557–581 / 550–577
Sui	581–618
Emperor Yang	605–617
Tang	618–907
Emperor Tai zong	627–649
Emperor Xuan zong	712–755
Five Dynasties	907–960
Later Shu	934–965
Southern Tang	937–976
Northern Song	960–1127
Emperor Tai zu	960–976
Emperor Tai zong	976–997

1

Documenting the loss

It is just over a thousand years since Zhao Kuangyi occupied the throne of China as Tai zong, second emperor of the Song dynasty. He ruled for twenty two years, from 976 to 997, and his reign began with a period bearing the title 'Supreme peace and nation restored' (*Taiping xingguo*). With the choice of this title he proclaimed a hopeful message: that a century of warfare and division, suffered since the dying years of the Tang dynasty and its collapse in 907, were now (or soon would be) resolved into the settled order of a new, unified regime.

Although I prefer to resist the banal language of 'turning points' and 'new eras', it is clear that for bibliographers this moment is at the heart of a really important period in Chinese history. Three developments stand out in it: the reassembling of an imperial library collection after the losses through war; the commissioning of three large encyclopedic compilations based on earlier literature; and China's transition from the manuscript age to the age of print. All three developments were intimately related together, all three had long-term implications reaching earlier and later than the tenth century, but it was Tai zong's reign that brought them into simultaneous focus. I want to look at them through Tai zong's eyes.

The scale of his problem in stocking the Three Institutes (*san guan*) which then formed the imperial library can be seen in both a short and a long perspective.

First, at the level of crude statistics, we can learn something of the tasks in hand from figures given in various documentary sources of the early Song. These medieval Chinese sources share a common characteristic in expressing the size of library holdings in numbers of scrolls. Throughout more than a thousand years of the manuscript age scrolls of paper or silk had been the basic physical unit of book production in China. Even when the age of print changed the physical reality by favouring the codex and other forms of book production, the terminology of scrolls remained indelibly associated with bibliographical usage – from then on as a textual unit akin to a chapter.

The early Song emperors belonged to the last generations for whom scrolls were still the standard form of books.[1] And when their dynasty was first proclaimed the imperial library possessed a mere twelve thousand of them.[2] Then, as the founding emperor Tai zu won control of the regional kingdoms of Jingnan (in 963) and Shu (965), he sent commissioners out there to recover books, documents and cultural objects, and that exercise brought in another thirteen thousand scrolls. Court officials donated more than a thousand to the throne in 966. And twenty thousand more followed when the Southern Tang submitted in 976.[3] All these were added to the collections in the Three Institutes. The running total, then, exceeded 46,000 scrolls.

Such was the situation that greeted Tai zong at the start of his reign in the same year. He responded first by building new and more spacious accommodation for the library, giving it a new title – the Court in Honour of Literature (*Chong wen yuan*), and adding a fourth unit, the Privy Gallery, which he used himself for personal reading.[4] Then, in 984, he instituted a search for books. At this point, remember, he had at least forty thousand scrolls – a figure which allows for duplication – by historic standards a decent-sized collection.[5] But Tai zong was not content with it. His comment was:

> Even though the books held in the Three Institutes are not few in number, if we consider the Kaiyuan catalogue the losses are still large. A wide search must be conducted.

And he gave his librarians a specific task:

> The books held in the Three Institutes must be compared and collated with the *Catalogue of books in four divisions* of the Kaiyuan period and a special search must be conducted for those seen to be missing. A full list should also be made of the missing books, with an announcement to all far and wide that if any government official's household has books which the Three Institutes lack, he is permitted to go to the Institutes and present them to the throne.

This edict of 984 added details of career and money inducements to encourage owners of missing books to come forward, and also alternative arrangements for copying texts whose owners preferred not to part with them.[6]

So Tai zong's mind was on the Kaiyuan period, 260 years before him, when the Tang emperor Xuan zong had been on the throne. He judged his own Three Institutes' collection ultimately against the huge descriptive catalogue which was compiled in that period under the title *A catalogue of all books, in four divisions*.[7] The total holding of scrolls recorded there in 721 was 51,852, and that excluded Buddhist and Daoist works, for which a separate catalogue was made, recording 9,500 scrolls of books.[8]

Beyond the sheer massing of numbers logged in the bureaucratic annals of the early Song there is an important point to observe. In improving his collection through a public search Tai zong used as his target a list of titles fixed back in the early eighth century: those were the books his officials were instructed to seek out, and those by implication were the books conspicuously missing from his current holdings. So, as we try to put ourselves in his shoes during the first years of his reign, we have to picture what the emperor himself described as a considerable collection of books that specialized in the more recent centuries following the great catalogue of 721. That was of course a period in which some of China's most significant literary, historical and intellectual writings had been achieved. Yet Tai zong seems to have felt no lack of those writings as he sought to bring his collection up to scratch. Apparently the books brought in during the 960s and 970s from cultural centres in the east and west were rich enough in holdings from the eighth, ninth and tenth centuries for him to leave that whole period out of his search. This important conclusion will come back into the picture later.

☆

Now is the moment to look at his collection-building in a longer perspective. Tai zong was not the first Chinese emperor to set about such a task. He belonged in that respect to a tradition which stretched back, again, a thousand years. He also inherited a tradition of critical bibliography and analytical catalogue work of equally impressive vintage.

Modern historians date the birth of Chinese bibliography to 6 BC, when an extended project to catalogue the imperial library of the Western Han dynasty took its final shape. The result was entitled *The seven summaries* (*Qi lue*), and behind it lay the labour of more than twenty years during which a member of the Han ruling house, the scholar Liu Xiang, with a small team of specialist collaborators, had worked through each book of the collection. He established authorship and text, organized the books systematically, wrote critical abstracts, then submitted the results item by item to the throne. The whole body of work was known as the *Separate transcripts* (*Bie lu*). When Liu Xiang died, his son Xin was given the task of compiling from this material the integrated catalogue which he submitted to the throne as *The seven summaries*. Both works have been lost for many centuries. But the classified list of titles from *The seven summaries* survives as a chapter in the official *History of the Han*, giving us a sharply focused view of the imperial collection two thousand years ago.[9]

The influence of this project reached on through the entire history of imperial bibliography, and in several distinct ways. First, the managing and documenting of book collections were sponsored by the throne and made the responsibility of high-ranking officers of state: in due course the Privy Directorate of Books (*Bi shu jian*) became and long remained a branch of the bureaucracy at the highest level, and was staffed accordingly.[10]

Secondly, the principle of subject classification was established right at the start, and although the system of classes used would evolve in both shape and specifics, the fundamentals laid down in *The seven summaries* have set a lasting pattern for later bibliographies. The Confucian scriptures stood apart at the head of the system; other distinct categories then followed – schools of philosophy; poetic literature; certain specialized fields of knowledge – military science, divination, medical techniques; each class then subdivided into sections to make, for its original purposes, a well articulated system. The third precedent set by this pioneer catalogue is more contextual: what began in conception and execution as a critical catalogue of an existing collection would find its way, condensed and transcribed, into the bibliographical monograph of a standard dynastic history. So a working catalogue was adapted to form a national bibliography and, forced through the strainer of history, would survive only in that heavily modified form. This pattern repeats itself, with more and more serious distortions, until quite recent times.

How the imperial library, with its staff, its premises, catalogues and classification schemes, evolved as a central institution of the Chinese state through the manuscript age – that story has been told elsewhere, and I'll not repeat it here.[11] But we ought to notice on this occasion how well the Chinese imperial state met the criteria described by Kenneth Humphreys in an earlier Panizzi Lecture series for what we now call a national library.[12] The Privy Directorate of Books was, as we have seen, funded and staffed by the state. It operated as a national bibliographical agency, concerned with strategic collection development and occupied with definitive catalogues and national bibliographies. The state library under the directorate's control was a treasury of historic documents and art-works. It was a symbol of national unity and culture, in the sense that it affirmed the ruling dynasty's legitimate inheritance and stewardship of written culture from the past. It also, of course, affirmed the ruling dynasty's central control over the whole sphere of written knowledge. In just two significant respects the Chinese state library failed to match the function of a modern national library: legal deposit and the provision of a central repository of information for citizen users are notions too recent, too egalitarian to make much sense in relation to China of the manuscript age. Yet even so, the second lecture in this series will find an individual scholar apparently using the state records for a personal project. All this means that China had most of the essential features of a national library in place and functioning for a clear millennium before the first tentative steps began in Europe.

These remarks on the long historical reach of *The seven summaries* project can bring us back to the Song and to Tai zong. When in 984 he looked to the authority of that eighth-century *Catalogue in four divisions* as a source reference for his own book search, he had more than a pragmatic need in mind. There was a sense of historic significance in looking back through time to the climax of the last major dynasty to rule all China, and to a period when the imperial collections had been more amply resourced than ever before. The catalogue which documented that richness was by then classified in four divisions – the final and permanent result of evolution from the Han classification – with Confucian Scriptures still first, then Histories, Masters, and Literary Collections. It had, as often before, been adapted for transcription as a bibliography into the official *History of the Tang* (*Jiu Tang shu*). And this work, completed in 945, came less than forty years before Tai zong's edict. So the Kaiyuan catalogue was accessible, was actually the most recent record of a major imperial library, but was symbolically also a statement of full imperial legitimacy which Tai zong was plainly striving to emulate.

What is missing from this modern, positive, results-driven view of Chinese bibliography is the sense of loss which was after all the strongest note sounded in Tai zong's edict of 984. That same note had echoed through the annals of bibliography from the earliest times. The *History of the Han*'s bibliographical monograph began its story with the stemming of wisdom at the deaths of Confucius and his seventy disciples, the disorder of learning in the political chaos of the following age, and the culminating act of the Qin emperor who, it says, 'destroyed literary compositions by burning and left the black-haired people in ignorance'.[13] For this and generations of later dynastic histories the Qin burning of the books in 213 BC was the decisive engine of library formation. In its wake the Han 'collected texts on a large scale and opened wide the way for writings to be offered up'. But that was only the first in a series of historical setbacks and disasters by which the legacy of books from the past was destroyed and had then to be restored by the following dynasty. The most eloquent statement of this cyclical process was a memorial presented to the Sui emperor in 583 by Niu Hong, as Privy Director of Books. He drew up a much quoted list of five book catastrophes, beginning with the Qin burning; then, in chronological sequence: the destruction by fire of the usurping ruler Wang Mang's palace during fighting in the capital city (AD 23); the loss of more than seventy cartloads of books during flight from the eastern to the western capital (AD 190); the fall and sack of the capital Loyang at the end of the Western Jin dynasty (311); and the wilful burning of the conquered Liang dynasty's collection by its emperor Yuan (555) – this last an event we shall look at more closely in the second lecture. Niu Hong's powerful memorial on the theme of loss was itself a spur for the Sui emperor to launch a new collection-building operation.[14]

The same litany of pain went on through the rest of imperial history. The early Tang Privy Directors of Books petitioned for new holdings to be gathered by purchase and donation in the wake of losses during the recent dynastic transition. The work of critical bibliographical review then began, to be taken up again a century later and lead to the catalogue of 721 which would in turn guide Tai zong's officers in the Song.[15] In due course the official history of the Song dynasty would once more refer to the Qin burning of books as the low point in history from which library collection would emerge.[16] And even in the thirties of the twentieth century a historian, Chen Dengyuan, used this same theme as his focus for a lengthy *Examination of the assembly and dispersal of texts ancient and modern*.[17]

Built into this permanent dynastic theme was the notion that the effort of recovery was a losing battle. With each new disaster a certain part of the legacy of past writings was irreplaceably gone. As time passed, more writings of early ages slipped beyond the horizon. The early catalogues themselves confronted later generations in detail with what had been lost. Even over the short range of one hundred years we see, for instance, the *History of the Sui* present in its bibliography a systematic annotation of recently missing books: it was completed in 656 on the basis of what was left of the Sui imperial library, but the compilers used catalogues from the Liang dynasty early in the previous century to identify titles recorded then but since lost. Although no later dynastic bibliography followed this example, search lists were later compiled of titles known to be missing after some episode of destruction. This was the case in 1144 and again in 1145 when efforts were being made to rebuild an imperial collection after the loss of north China and sack of the northern capital Kaifeng in 1127.[18]

A global view expressed in the mid-twelfth century estimated, no doubt with some hyperbole, that 'less than one or two percent' of books from the past survived into that time.[19] In turn, an estimate in the late seventeenth century, looking back to the same time, found that 'from the Song until the present there have been more than ten catalogues – a brilliant spectacle; but if you seek out the actual books, less than forty or fifty percent survive.' Writing more than two hundred years later in 1936, Chen Dengyuan was quite content to extrapolate from that.[20]

Such despairing rhetoric of loss ultimately owed its energy to the system of moral and intellectual authority in Confucian China, where the fundamental values of public and private life were derived from teachings of ancient sages, precariously and imperfectly transmitted in canonical texts. It also implied a certain theory or rationale of loss. According to this view books survived if they were held in (or could be recovered for) the imperial collections; if not, they were lost. But paper scrolls held in the wooden structures of imperial libraries were virtually by definition condemned to destruction, whether through political violence or through mishap by fire. Hence the downward spiral through a succession of dynasties.

This stark and simple view lacks explanatory power. Why were some ancient texts successfully transmitted through the ages and others not? It also fails to acknowledge the state's own active role in promoting or eliminating certain classes of books.

The First Qin Emperor was not the only ruler of China to conduct a selective purge of literature. The Sui Emperor Yang, who came to the throne in AD 605, launched a root-and-branch campaign to burn a whole class of literature – the apocryphal texts, associated with Confucian scriptures, which represented traditions of political prophecy. The campaign extended throughout society, wielding the sanction of death, and left the imperial collection itself heavily depleted.[21] (In fact the Song emperor Tai zong himself would show the same hostility to the politically threatening skills of diviners: in one of the early acts of his reign he confiscated texts used by diviners throughout the land.[22]) A more subtle intervention in the record of transmission was frankly stated in the *History of the Sui*, at the opening of its bibliographical monograph: certain items included in previous catalogues were now deleted on grounds of literary quality or moral value; others, absent from older catalogues, were now introduced on similar grounds.[23] It becomes clear that the imperial bibliographies, whatever the nature of their links to real collections in imperial libraries, bore a much more problematic relationship to books in currency at large in society.

In the mid-twelfth century a new voice spoke out on these matters, giving a very different analysis. It was the voice of Zheng Qiao (1104–1162), a man who devoted much of his energies in life to a large-scale history of China before the Tang, the *General record* (*Tong zhi*). Into this work he incorporated the results of some years of bibliographical study: his *Composite account of all books* (*Qun shu hui ji*), now lost, was adapted to form a monograph in the *General record*. The monograph has attracted criticism for the author's reliance on existing catalogues and his failure to base conclusions on direct study of the books in his list.[24] But his more radical thoughts on bibliographical matters appear in another monograph headed 'Textual collation' (*Jiao chou lüe*), which expressly addresses the question of books lost to transmission.

Zheng Qiao has one central insight to offer: that survival and loss of books from the past must be seen as part of one same process, and that transmission is more central to the problem than destruction. His argument goes like this. Even during the

Qin dynasty, when Confucian books had notoriously been burned and scholars put to the sword, the traditions of Confucian scholarship were maintained by certain individuals and their followers. The Qin administration itself made use of books and documents: its purge was a single episode, not to be held responsible for the many losses which took place before and after it. Certain parts of the Confucian texts were lost despite the Qin, not because of it. What secures the survival of learning in transmitted books is the existence of specialist traditions of knowledge: specialists make it their business to copy and transmit the books which carry their learning. That is why the traditions of medicine, of Buddhism and of Daoism have survived the turbulence and destruction of history, while the rich Han literature on the *Book of changes* and the Legalist school has largely been lost. Only by making specialisms clear through systematic classification can the full corpus of books be grasped and thus preserved. It is important to keep records of lost books, to make search lists, to have coherent accounts of integral traditions of learning. Comprehensive information like that will inform the search for books which can often be recovered from open society, but gaps in the record will lead to actual loss. Muddled classification creates the same risk. There lies the importance of critical collation, which alone ensures that every book finds its rightful place in the system. Certain apparently lost books can actually be recovered indirectly from the contents of other, transmitted, texts. Certain ancient schools of knowledge still have books in currency which fail to appear in recent catalogues. There are even books which failed to appear in catalogues of their own time, only to surface in later lists. Meanwhile the search for lost books at large in society needs to proceed on rational principles: by identifying the specialists in related fields of knowledge, seeking out regional specialisms and private family traditions, looking for institutional material in administrative offices, winning the confidence of private collectors, exploiting personal connections, and taking heed of recent books in currency before the passage of time puts them beyond reach.

I have paraphrased an argument which runs over several pages densely sown with examples, some of them more impressive than others. Zheng Qiao's monograph goes on from here to develop a detailed critique of blunders in the recent catalogues of the mid-twelfth century that he was using. But for bibliographers to this day his basic point will still ring a bell. There is surely something inescapable in his reasoning that books will survive only if someone is committed enough to make copies of them. Throughout history, until the invention of the photocopying machine, to copy a book has required investment of time, skilled labour and money. If no-one has the motivation for that, the book cannot expect to survive the moment of physical destruction. That is why the disasters befalling imperial libraries through time are no more than secondary causes of book loss: real loss occurs when the search in open society finds no copies in transmission.

Zheng Qiao shows a lively sense of the rich book resources to be found out there in society. He writes of a Daoist priest who had a full set of literary collections by Tang authors, of a Buddhist monk with a collection of work by all the famous Song calligraphers. But a more revealing observation is the example of 'Targeting under cover' (*she fu*), a branch of divination which was once used in a kind of ritual game: competitors had to work their divining arts to discover the identity of objects kept under cover. Zheng Qiao observes: 'the school was there in Han times, and its books are current in society now; but the bibliography of the *[New] history of the Tang* and the *Catalogue [of the Court] in Honour of Literature* have nothing of them at all.'[25] We saw just now that imperial regimes had looked sternly on diviners and their books for centuries before this: it's not surprising that imperial catalogues ignored them now. But if Zheng Qiao was right in contending that *she fu* texts were still at large in society,[26] then his main point finds its clinching proof: even government suppression would not wipe out a tradition of books in the hands of committed practitioners. (The third lecture in this series will revisit the game of 'Targeting under cover' in another context.)

A preoccupation with subject classification as the solution to all ills of book transmission still raises problems. Zheng Qiao expressly compares clarity in classification to military discipline:

just as well-disciplined troops will win out over poorly disciplined troops, so will well-classified books survive better than poorly classified books. Good order enables large collections, like large bodies of troops, to be kept under control; lack of order creates confusion even among small numbers. With this principle Zheng has embraced the thinking of the imperial state. For him categories are vital not simply because they identify active, self-perpetuating specialisms, but also because they fit into a single, overall system. And the master of that system has power over all knowledge: every activity within it must fit at his bidding into a subordinate place. Even though, as Zheng Qiao observes, given imperial catalogues might omit or muddle up particular categories, that is merely bad practice. His vision of the perfect classification, good for all time, is like a great machine with all its tiny individual parts whirring and buzzing away. Damage and loss occur only when particular units in the system run out of steam.

The problem here is that classification systems are intellectual, and fundamentally also political, constructs: they represent, and impose, a view of the world at a certain time and in a certain environment.[27] But the creation of books throughout history obeys different dynamics and rarely sits easily within the classifiers' systems. Intellectual life moves on, old schools fade away, new schools emerge. Yet Zheng Qiao, alive though he was to book culture as a living presence in the society of his own day, did not distance himself from the centralizing force of imperial tradition. He submitted his bibliographical work to the throne in 1149 and completed his *General record* as an official of the crown in 1161.[28]

All this gives some perspective on Song Tai zong's position as he came to the throne in the late tenth century. His inherited collection of books, he said himself, was 'not small' in size, but assembled unsystematically from varied sources. It was apparently stronger in titles from recent centuries than in the mainstream from the past. He aspired to develop it into a collection that would match the high point of the Tang and he took his guidance from the published imperial catalogue of that period, with its traditional classification. His perception of book loss and his strategies of book recovery conformed entirely to ancient models.

But to conclude from this that he knew and cared nothing about new developments in book culture would be wrong. His century was the time when wood-block printing had moved beyond its origins in Buddhist and Daoist ritual practice and early forms of popular publication. As a technology for serious book production it was past the experimental stage. Already a state-sponsored set of Confucian scriptures had been printed under the Later Tang kingdom between 932 and 953.[29] In the kingdom of Shu a private individual, Wu Zhaoyi, had sponsored the printing of certain standard literary and reference works around the middle of the century, followed by a further set of Confucian texts launched with royal approval in the 950s.[30] There is evidence that blocks prepared for these editions were among the books and objects brought from Shu to the Song court in 966.[31]

The early Song emperors took up the new technology with enthusiasm, and their dynasty was to preside over the first great flowering of Chinese printing. Tai zong's brother, the founding Song emperor Tai zu, had commissioned a first printing of the Buddhist canon in 971. The engraved blocks of this edition, prepared in the regional capital of Shu, would be delivered to the throne during Tai zong's reign, in 983.[32] Meanwhile the new dynasty was building a printed corpus of standard commentaries to the Confucian scriptures.[33] Amid this large-scale programme to produce definitive printed versions of Confucian and Buddhist texts, the first frankly secular work to be printed by imperial command was entitled *Extensive records for the time of Supreme Peace* (*Taiping guang ji*). The printing was ordered in 981, but the order to compile it had been issued in 977, only months after Tai zong had come to the throne, and the finished work was submitted to him and deposited in the Institute of History during 978.[34]

This now famous collection of prose narrative, comprising

five hundred scroll/chapters, was a companion set to go with an even larger compilation commissioned at the same time, the *Imperial reader for the time of Supreme Peace* (*Taiping yu lan*) in one thousand scroll/chapters. The *Imperial reader* was completed and presented to the throne by the start of 984.[35] And a third great compilation had been commissioned in 982, the *Finest blooms in the garden of letters* (*Wen yuan ying hua*), also in one thousand scroll/chapters; it was finished in 987.[36]

Logging the years in which these literary compilations were commissioned, completed, and in one case printed, brings out their place in the broader picture. Tai zong in the first years of his reign was simultaneously rehousing his imperial library, exploiting the technology of wood-block printing, and creating a textual corpus of material extracted from past literature. For us, as we try to learn more about the lost books of medieval China, that combination of circumstances carries a clear message: the compilations of Tai zong's reign were put together almost entirely in the years *before* the expansion of the Three Institutes' collection. The editorial teams who worked on them had at their disposal no more than the collection of 40,000 scrolls inherited from Tai zu's reign, conspicuously weak in titles older than the eighth century. That is the angle from which we should prepare to search their work for the text of early books.

The three compilations, transmitted to our own time, have become great gates through which we can contemplate a largely vanished literature from ancient and medieval China – something which has been appreciated since at least the twelfth century.[37] And, particularly since the sixteenth century, editors and scholars have readily come forward to work through them for textual material to reconstruct lost ancient books.[38] This has given substance to Zheng Qiao's argument that some lost texts can be recovered indirectly from the contents of other, transmitted, texts. But the compilations of Tai zong's reign each present a distinct set of problems which complicate the work of reconstruction in theory and in practice. The business of these lectures from here on will be to grapple with those problems.

To deal with the last title first: the *Finest blooms in the garden of literature* will not occupy us much in what follows. It is for sure an incomparably rich source of texts in prose and verse from the formal literature of the Tang period: they make up nine tenths of its bulk. But it cites no sources. Instead each poem, essay, letter or inscription appears as a discrete textual item, with only its author and title to identify it. Without more pedigree than that, the material has value for textual editors, but not for reconstructive bibliographers. Except that it does substantially confirm the impression that the compilers in the 970s and 980s had access to a fine collection of Tang literature.

Things are different with the two other compilations, *Imperial reader* and *Extensive records*. They were both commissioned simultaneously by the same edict in 977, and made the responsibility of the same editorial board of senior officials. The terms of that commission are important for grasping the use of sources in each case. For one project (the *Imperial reader*) it prescribed three named literary encyclopedias of former generations, and 'books in general' (*zhu shu*), for classification and compiling into one thousand scroll/chapters.[39] For the companion project (*Extensive records*) it called for informal histories, transmitted records, stories and commonplaces to be made into an assorted compilation of five hundred scroll/chapters.[40] In each case both the targeted sources and the expected products look, at first sight, very different. But the reality is that the editorial board, which no doubt gave the actual work to teams of junior, unnamed personnel, had to produce their results from the same imperial collection. Its characteristics must be reflected in those results.

The *Imperial reader* that comes down to us is a general encyclopedia classed in fifty five subject sections, each one finely subdivided into particular topics. The text is a dense sequence of quotations from named sources. But in terms of bibliographical value these source references bristle with problems. In very many cases they name only an author and an individual literary composition, giving no book source. In many others they do name a book title, which has made it possible to index the whole work in a way that reassembles the quotations ascribed to each source. But that still leaves open the underlying question: how much of the material comes directly from the cited source-texts, how much is merely copied from older generations of encyclopedias?

There was a time, and it lasted for centuries, when users of the *Imperial reader* thought that everything came from original books, and that the work thus gave an index of which books survived in the late tenth century.[41] But when the text of the commissioning decree was traced and republished in the 1930s,[42] opinion swung heavily to the opposite side. For didn't that decree expressly require the *Imperial reader* to be compiled from named encyclopedias? And evidence is easy to find of confusion and inconsistency arising from indiscriminate copying of older compilations, themselves indebted to yet earlier compilations reaching back centuries in time.[43] Still, there is a trap here. Of the three specified source-encyclopedias only one, the shortest, survives.[44] We can't verify on any useful scale how much text in the *Imperial reader* was drawn from them. But we do know that the latest of those three sources was created in 641. If everything had been copied from them, the *Imperial reader* would contain no material later than that date.[45] Whatever later material it does contain necessarily comes from elsewhere. The text of the commission edict is vague on this matter, but its effect is clear. It created two time zones: one earlier than 641, for which the compilers were told to use the three encyclopedias, the other later than 641, for which they enjoyed open season on anything they found in the library. And this later period was, allowing for a few years' gap, well covered in Tai zong's collection. If the *Imperial reader* did quote from works of the eighth century and later, there is a good chance that real books lay behind the quotations.

The team working on the *Extensive records* enjoyed even wider scope. The commission edict turned them loose on a broadly defined literature of informal, anecdotal narrative. They produced the results with great despatch in less than eighteen months – five hundred scroll/chapters, classified by subject, reflecting an overall interest in topics unorthodox and marginal to public concerns. The stories themselves are self-contained units that vary in length, but are usually quite short. Editorial policy was to name a textual source – briefly, it's true – but usually with enough precision to identify a bibliographical item.

This collection opens up a body of medieval literature which would otherwise scarcely come to our notice. Appreciable numbers of its source-titles make no appearance in imperial bibliographies. But a problem lies concealed in those inviting characteristics. Where so much is uniquely transmitted and presented in such seamless fashion, how are we to judge the integrity of quotation? In my experience modern editors have often been lured by the rich abundance of remarkable narrative prose into simply embracing the text they receive from the *Extensive records* as authoritative. The reality is almost certainly more messy. When, occasionally, comparison with parallel texts is possible, it shows up gaps, simplifications and misattributions in the *Extensive records*. Flaws like these could certainly be explained by haste. But the same underlying question comes up as before: how much secondary quotation from flawed encyclopedic sources is going on here? And the same general observation applies: the more recent in time the quoted sources are, the more genuine a chance we have that the quotations draw directly upon the named books themselves.

In fact both the *Imperial reader* and the *Extensive records* make generous use of material from the eighth, ninth and tenth centuries. They use some books that were only a few years old when the compilations were made. Both quote from the first *History of the Tang* (945) and from the collected institutional records of that dynasty known as *Tang hui yao* (961). The *Imperial reader* quotes from the first *History of the Five Dynasties* (completed in 974, less than ten years before the *Imperial reader* itself), and the *Extensive records* actually uses a book by a member of its own editorial board, Xu Xuan (917–992).[46] Both collections quote from tenth-century books originating in the kingdom of Shu,[47] which suggests that these titles were among the holdings acquired from that kingdom when it was annexed in 965. But the broader pattern is more telling: if we identify those titles in each collection which fall after the year 721 – the date of the

Kaiyuan catalogue – we find more than 140 in the *Imperial reader*, perhaps 10 percent of the total, and 190 in the *Extensive records*, about 40 percent of the total. These are the books which most deserve to attract the attention of reconstructing editors, and, in the case of the *Extensive records*, so they have. But not with the *Imperial reader*, where the reconstructors have shown much greater interest in early texts, taking their chances with the long trails of derived quotations which separate them from the ancient originals.

☆

These questions of authority and authenticity are dauntingly obscure, and our grasp of them is still at a primitive level. But they are not trivial, and I want to suggest that the very basis of our understanding of medieval literature is at stake here.

Books survive through time when later generations have reason to copy and hand them on. They are continually changed by this process – crudely and blatantly through corruption and revision; more subtly through the handling of textual presentation and the accretion of prefaces, commentaries, and illustrations; most subtly of all through the changing mindset of those who read them and find there what they want to read.[48] The very opposite things are true of books that are lost. Lacking the power to motivate copying and transmission in later times – which from the tenth century on often meant the cutting of printing blocks – they either vanish altogether or stay on, set in amber, as textual fragments in other collections. There they keep some remnants of distinctive, even parochial characteristics from the time when they still survived, the very qualities which students of the past should prize the most.

That is why I have described the *Imperial reader* and the *Extensive records* as gateways to lost medieval literature. Through them we can reach out towards certain books that still existed in Tai zong's state library of the late tenth century. What exactly we find there, how we deal with it, how much remains finally beyond our grasp – these matters will be probed and tested on actual examples in the two lectures which follow.

The library itself, about which so much has been said here, lasted one more generation. Then, in the great fire of 1015, it went up in flames.

NOTES

1 The tangible demonstration of this is the corpus of books sealed in cave 17 at Dunhuang in the opening years of the eleventh century: see comments by Fujieda Akira in 'The Tunhuang manuscripts, a general description', *Zinbun* (Memoirs of the Research Institute for Humanistic Studies, Kyoto University) No. 9, 1966, pp. 16 ff. Figures given by Jean-Pierre Drège identify 166 books in codex form in the Stein collection, 120 in the Pelliot collection (both figures including works in Tibetan), one in Beijing, and some 60 in St Petersburg. These represent a tiny element among the many thousands of scrolls in the whole corpus: see 'Les cahiers des manuscrits de Touen-houang', in Michel Soymié, ed., *Contributions aux études sur Touen-houang*, Geneva and Paris 1979, p. 17. Drège, *ibid*., documents the twentieth-century literature on the gradual evolution of the physical form of Chinese books. The same author has discussed other book forms recovered from Dunhuang in 'Les accordéons de Dunhuang', in Michel Soymié, ed., *Contributions aux études sur Touen-houang, Volume III*, Paris 1984, pp. 195–204; and 'Papillons et tourbillons', in J-P. Drège, ed., *De Dunhuang au Japon: études chinoises et bouddhiques offertes à Michel Soymié*, Geneva 1996, pp. 163–178.

2 *Xu zi zhi tong jian chang bian* 續資治通鑒長編, by Li Dao 李燾 (1115–1184), Beijing 1979–1995, 19.422; *Song shi* 宋史, Beijing 1977, 202.5032. The figure was 13,000 according to *Huang chao lei yuan* 皇朝類苑, 1911 ed., 31.4a, and *Song hui yao ji gao* 宋會要輯稿, Taibei 1976: *Chong ru* 崇儒, 4.15a.

3 *Song hui yao ji gao: Chong ru*, 4.15a; *Huang chao lei yuan* 31.4a. A translation by Robert des Rotours of the relevant passage appears

in Paul Pelliot, *Les débuts de l'imprimerie en Chine*, Paris 1953, p. 72, n. 1. The formal submission of the Southern Tang took place on Kaibao 開寶 8/11/27 [1 January 976]: see *Xu zi zhi tong jian chang bian* 16.352.

4 *Xu zi zhi tong jian chang bian* 19.422, for Taiping xingguo 太平興國 3/2/1 [12 March 978]; *Song shi* 202.5032.

5 The official tally, covering duplicate copies of books, was 80,000 scrolls. See last note, and *Huang chao lei yuan* 31.4a.

6 Edict of Taiping xingguo 9/1/*renxu* 壬戌 [15 February 984]: *Tai zong huangdi shilu* 太宗皇帝實錄, in *Sibu congkan* 四部叢刊 Third Series, 28.2b–3a; cf. *Song hui yao ji gao: Chong ru*, 4.16ab; *Xu zi zhi tong jian chang bian* 25.571. An earlier search launched in 977/10 had focused strongly on items of classic calligraphy: *Song hui yao ji gao: Chong ru*, 4.15b.

7 *Qun shu si bu lu* 群書四部錄, in 200 scrolls, completed in 721. This was later digested by Wu Jiong 毋煚 into a shorter catalogue of 40 scrolls, the *Catalogue of books ancient and modern* (*Gu jin shu lu* 古今書錄), which in turn was the basis of the summary catalogue reproduced in the bibliographical chapters of *Jiu Tang shu* 舊唐書. See *Jiu Tang shu*, Beijing 1975, 46.1962. The title 'Catalogue of books in four divisions of the Kaiyuan period' as used by Tai zong 太宗 is very likely a reference to Wu Jiong's *Gu jin shu lu*, which survived into the eleventh century: on this point, see Piet van der Loon, *Taoist books in the libraries of the Sung period: a critical study and index*, London 1984, p. 9, n. 26.

8 The *Kaiyuan catalogue of inner and outer scriptures* (*Kaiyuan nei wai jing lu* 開元內外經錄), in 10 scrolls, was also by Wu Jiong: *Jiu Tang shu* 46.1965.

9 *Han shu* 漢書, Beijing 1962, 30.1701–81. The total number of scrolls recorded is 3,269.

10 The *Bi shu jian* 秘書監 was first instituted under the Later Han dynasty, in the reign of emperor Huan [AD 147–167]. Its title mutated through various forms under successive dynasties until the Yuan.
11 Jean-Pierre Drège, *Les bibliothèques en Chine au temps des manuscrits (jusqu'au Xe siècle)*, Paris 1991.
12 K. W. Humphreys, *A national library in theory and in practice*, (Panizzi Lectures 1987), London 1988. For the features listed below, see pp. 2 (funded by the state), 8, 23 (responsibility of the state; open to the public; symbol of national unity), 38 (national bibliographic agency).
13 *Han shu* 30.1701.
14 *Sui shu* 隋書, Beijing 1973, 49.1297–1300.
15 On early Tang collection and catalogue work see *Jiu Tang shu* 46.1962.
16 *Song shi* 202.5032.
17 Chen Dengyuan 陳登原, *Gujin dianji ju san kao* 古今典籍聚散考, Shanghai 1936.
18 A skeleton version (1144) of the large descriptive catalogue *Chong wen zong mu* 崇文總目, and its sequel entitled *Bi shu sheng xu bian dao si ku que shu mu* 秘書省續編到四庫闕書目 (1145), have both come down to us. They are discussed in detail by Piet van der Loon, *Taoist books*, pp. 6–7, 12–15.
19 *Tong zhi* 通志, by Zheng Qiao 鄭樵, Zhejiang shuju edition, 1896, 71.1b.
20 *Liu tong gu shu yue* 流通古書約, by Cao Rong 曹溶 (1613–1685), in *Zhi bu zu zhai congshu* 知不足齋叢書, Series 40, 1a. Compare Chen Dengyuan, p. 1.
21 *Sui shu* 32.941. The passage actually traces imperial suppression of these texts back to the Southern Dynasties: the Daming 大明

period of Song 宋 (457–464) and Tianjian 天監 period of the Liang 梁 (502–519).

22 *Xu zi zhi tong jian chang bian* 18.414, for Taiping xingguo 2/10/*bingzi* 丙子 [2 December 977].

23 *Sui shu* 32.908.

24 For a fuller statement of the points sketched in this paragraph, see van der Loon, *Taoist books*, pp. 15–17.

25 *Tong zhi* 71.8b. The practice of *she fu* 射覆 as a court game is documented from the second century BC down to the third century AD: see references in *Han shu* 65.2843–4, 2874; *San guo zhi* 三國志, Beijing 1959, 29.817 and n. 1; 823, n. 1; 827–8, n. 1; *Jin shu* 晉書, Beijing 1974, 95.2479. Books with this expression in their title are listed in *Sui shu* 34.1032 (from a Liang catalogue) and 1034. The *Jiu Tang shu*, 14.405, records the dismissal in 786 of forty two specialist practitioners in the Hanlin Academy, including *she fu* among physiognomists, stargazers and others. Cf. also *Jin shi* 金史, Beijing 1975, 126.2740 and *Qing shi gao* 清史稿, Beijing 1977, 484.13354.

26 Three titles related to *she fu* would later appear in the bibliography of *Song shi*, 206.5242, which drew upon bibliographies in the sequence of national histories compiled under the Song, but added other material. See van der Loon, *Taoist books in the libraries of the Sung period*, p. 20.

27 Drège, *Les bibliothèques en Chine*, pp. 89–91, discusses the point in relation to medieval China.

28 *Jiaji yi gao* 夾漈遺稿, in *Yi hai zhu chen* 藝海珠塵, 2.3b–5b; *Song shi* 436.12944; *Jianyan yi lai xi nian yao lu* 建炎以來繫年要錄, Beijing 1988, 178.2942, 179.2958. See van der Loon, *Taoist books*, p. 15.

29 *Ce fu yuan gui* 冊府元龜, 1642 edn. repr. Beijing 1960, 608.29b–31a. Pelliot's detailed study of this episode appears in *Les débuts de l'imprimerie en Chine*, pp. 50–54.

30 For Pelliot's study of Wu Zhaoyi's woodblock printed books, see *Les débuts de l'imprimerie en Chine*, pp. 61–81. Other cases of private printing in the tenth century are discussed, *ibid.*, pp. 83–5.

31 *Ibid.*, pp. 75–6, citing *Jiao shi bi sheng* 焦氏筆乘 by Jiao Hong 焦竑 (1541–1620), in *Yue ya tang congshu* 粵雅堂叢書, 4.19.

32 *Fo zu tong ji* 佛祖統記, no. 2035 in *Taishō shinshu issaikyō* 大正新修大藏經, Tokyo 1924–1935, vol. 49, 43.396a and 398c. Pelliot, pp. 88–9; Demiéville, *ibid*, pp. 121ff.

33 *Yu hai* 玉海 (repr. by Wenwu chubanshe, Beijing 1987) 43.11a, 15a, 16a; *Song shi* 287.9656. This evidence is summarized by Pelliot, pp. 86–8.

34 *Taiping guang ji* 太平廣記, repr. Beijing 1959/1961: memorial of submission to the throne.

35 Edict of Taiping xingguo 8/11/*gengchen* 庚辰 [4 January 984]: see *Tai zong huangdi shilu* 27.5a. The work first bore the title *Taiping zonglei* 太平總類, which was changed to *Taiping yu lan* 太平御覽 in an edict of Taiping xingguo 8/12/*gengzi* 庚子 [24 January 984]: see *Tai zong huangdi shilu* 27.7a.

36 *Yu hai* 54.17a, quoting [*Song*] *hui yao*. Cf *Song hui yao ji gao: Chong ru* 5.1a.

37 Hong Mai 洪邁 (1123–1202) in *Rong zhai wu bi* 容齋五筆, Shanghai 1978 ed. of *Rong zhai sui bi* 容齋隨筆, 7.884–5 ('Guo chu wen ji' 國初文籍) remarks that of 1690 titles cited in *Taiping yu lan* 太平御覽, 70 or 80 percent were already lost to transmission. Chen Dengyuan, *Gujin dianji ju san kao*, pp. 208–9, accepts this as a measure of book loss between the Northern and Southern Song, a point which will need correction below.

38 Some of that work is discussed by Rudolf G. Wagner, 'Twice removed from the truth: fragment collection in 18th and 19th century China', in Glenn W. Most, ed., *Collecting fragments: Fragmente sammeln*, Göttingen 1997, pp. 34–52.

39 This is the version of the commission transcribed from [*Tai zong huangdi*] *shi lu* in *Yu hai* 54.34a. The phrase 'books in general' (諸書) appears differently, as 'encyclopedias of former ages' (前代類書) in the simplified version transcribed from *Song chao yao lu* 宋朝要錄 in *Xu zi zhi tong jian chang bian* 18.401.

40 *Yu hai* 54.34ab, quoting [*Tai zong huangdi*] *shilu*; cf. *Xu zi zhi tong jian chang bian* 18.401, quoting *Song chao yao lu*.

41 See above, n. 37. Hong Mai's figure of 1690 titles comes from a general list of sources appended at the head of the work at some point later in time. This includes book titles and authors, but not individual compositions. But it overlooks a multitude of duplications and variants and therefore considerably overstates the total. See Nie Chongqi 聶崇岐, preface to *Taiping yu lan yinde* 太平御覽引得, Harvard-Yenching Sinological Index Series, Index no. 23, Beijing 1935 [repr. Taibei 1966], pp. vii–viii.

42 By Deng Siyu 鄧嗣禹 in *Taiping guang ji pianmu ji yinshu yinde* 太平廣記篇目及引書引得, Harvard-Yenching Sinological Index Series, Index no. 15, Beijing 1934 [repr. Taibei 1966], pp. V–VI and Nie Chongqi, *Taiping yu lan yinde*, p. i.

43 Nie Chongqi, *Taiping yu lan yinde*, pp. x–xii; followed by John Winthrop Haeger, 'The significance of confusion: the origins of the T'ai-p'ing yü-lan', *Journal of the American Oriental Society* 88, 1968, pp. 405–6.

44 The *Classified assembly of literature* (*Yi wen lei ju* 藝文類聚) of 624, in one hundred scroll/chapters.

45 In fact two contemporary scholars have unaccountably made this claim, despite the evidence of the collection itself: Harold D. Roth, *The textual history of the* Huai-nan Tzu, Ann Arbor 1992, pp. 54 and 91; Robert Ford Campany, *Strange writing: anomaly accounts in early medieval China*, Albany 1996, p. 33, n. 22.

46 *Ji shen lu* 稽神錄.

47 Titles by Du Guangting 杜光庭 (850–933), Daoist divine at the court of Wang Jian 王建, first king of Shu 蜀: *Yongcheng ji xian lu* 墉城集仙錄, *Lu yi ji* 錄異記, *Shen xian gan tong lu* 神仙感通錄, *Qiu ran ke zhuan* 虯髯客傳, *Xian zhuan shi yi* 仙傳拾遺: all quoted in *Taiping guang ji*, the first two also in *Taiping yu lan*. Title by Jin Liyong 金利用: *Yu xi bian shi* 玉溪編事. Title by Zhou Ting 周挺: *Jing jie lu* 警誡錄. Title by He Guangyuan 何光遠: *Jian jie lu* 鑒戒錄.

48 In making this observation I am conscious of following arguments developed by earlier Panizzi Lecturers – Donald F. McKenzie, *Bibliography and the sociology of texts*, The 1985 Panizzi Lectures, London 1986, p. 20, echoed by Roger Chartier, 'Gutenberg revisited from the East', *Late Imperial China* 17.1, 1996, p. 6.

Reconstruction: the case of *Summary documents of three kingdoms*

A SIMPLE WAY TO THINK about books is to divide them into two sorts: transmitted and lost. But that is too simple. For one thing, books are always migrating from one category to the other: all books are transmitted down to a certain point in time before, in many cases, they vanish from sight; and conversely, the fortunes of discovery often mean that even lost books can re-emerge from long periods of obscurity. But my last lecture made a further point, that in China very many books from the past exist in a state which is neither full transmission nor full loss. If we want to pursue those books by probing beyond the intermediate sources more deeply into the past, we have to face the task of reconstruction, entailing as it does questions which are both practical and theoretical, and ultimately even philosophical.

This is an important part of our study of China, and one which deserves more attention that it normally gets. We too easily agree to form our perceptions of China's literature and history from a canon of books which owe their canonization to the fact that they *are* transmitted. But what about the books that were not? Were they not part of Chinese literature too? I have argued that transmission itself is not a wholly random process, by which some books happen to succumb to destruction and neglect, while others happen luckily to escape those fates. Books are transmitted only because someone wants to transmit them. If no-one is interested in taking that trouble with a particular book, it just will not survive. Which clearly means that transmission over long periods of time reflects an equally long series of positive value-judgements, or investment decisions, about the books in transmission, and only the books which stand that series of tests will make it to our time. Of course they will do this entirely on the terms of those who decide to transmit them, in whose power we also lie.

But we are here to talk about the lost books. The failure of later times to deliver them to us through normal means of transmission is not a matter of indifference, but rather a profoundly interesting circumstance. It actually guarantees that they had about them something peculiar to their own age that distinguished them from the ages which followed. They fell out of fashion and favour. So the enterprise of recovering them has the clear aim to find out that peculiarity and distinctiveness, and to sharpen and enrich our perceptions of intellectual life in those earlier times. In this enterprise our value-judgements matter little: bad or unpopular books from a remote time make just as desirable objects of recovery as good.

To demonstrate the challenges and rewards of textual recovery I am going to follow through a working example chosen from the corpus of lost books described in the last lecture. Appearing just too late for inclusion in the great catalogue of 721, this book evidently did survive to form part of Tai zong's collection in 976, and indeed seems to have survived in fragmentary form at least until 1178. It was excerpted for quotation in the imperial compilations commissioned in 977 – *Extensive records for the time of Supreme Peace* and *Imperial reader for the time of Supreme Peace*. Its entries in two critical catalogues of the Northern Song imperial libraries have mercifully survived for us to study. And since this was a historical text we also have opportunities for textual comparison: there are fully transmitted parallel histories which drew upon the same original documentary sources; and another important transmitted work in turn drew directly upon the target book itself. These are the bibliographical resources which sinological scholarship can muster and deploy to reconstruct a book lost for nearly a thousand years.[1]

The name of this book is *Summary documents of three kingdoms*. It was written around the start of the eighth century by a man called Qiu Yue. And it was a history of the mid-sixth century – the last fifty years of the Northern and Southern Dynasties period, leading up to the point when the empire was unified in readiness for the Tang dynasty under which Qiu Yue himself lived.

Let me clear up at once an obvious puzzle about the title *Three Kingdoms*, and refresh your picture of what was going on. This was not the famous three-zone China that developed at the end of the Han. It was an unstable China of the sixth century, in which shifting patterns of power moved between three main regions – the north-west, the central plain/north-east, and the south.

Various different power transfers were under way. In 534 what had once been the Northern Wei dynasty (under non-Chinese rulers, the Tuoba) split into two regions, Eastern and Western. That split marks the moment at which Qiu Yue would open his history. Later the Western Wei gave way to the Northern Zhou (also ruled by a northern tribal family, the Xianbei, surnamed Yuwen), and the Eastern Wei to the Northern Qi (whose rulers' surname was Gao). And meanwhile the long and splendid reign of emperor Wu and his Liang dynasty in the south (ruled by a Chinese royal house) suffered a destructive rebellion led by Hou Jing (548), followed soon after by the loss of capital and emperor to invading troops from the Western Wei (555). A remnant of the Liang ended up as a small dependency on a pocket of land within the territory of the Northern Zhou. What remained of the south passed under the rule of the Chen. And in the north the Zhou proceeded to conquer the Northern Qi. That was the scene when the first Sui emperor took charge in 581, starting by taking power from the

Three Kingdoms from 534

Zhou and moving on to unify the empire. And that too was when the curtain fell in Qiu Yue's book.

This half-century of warfare saw some of the most spectacular, tragic and appalling events in Chinese history, and the rulers of the Tang dynasty were intensely interested in it. They needed to be sure they understood the lessons it had to teach them about security and stability, so that they wouldn't share the fate of the Sui, which lasted a mere twenty years before its fall. So in the seventh century the Tang emperor Tai zong commissioned a

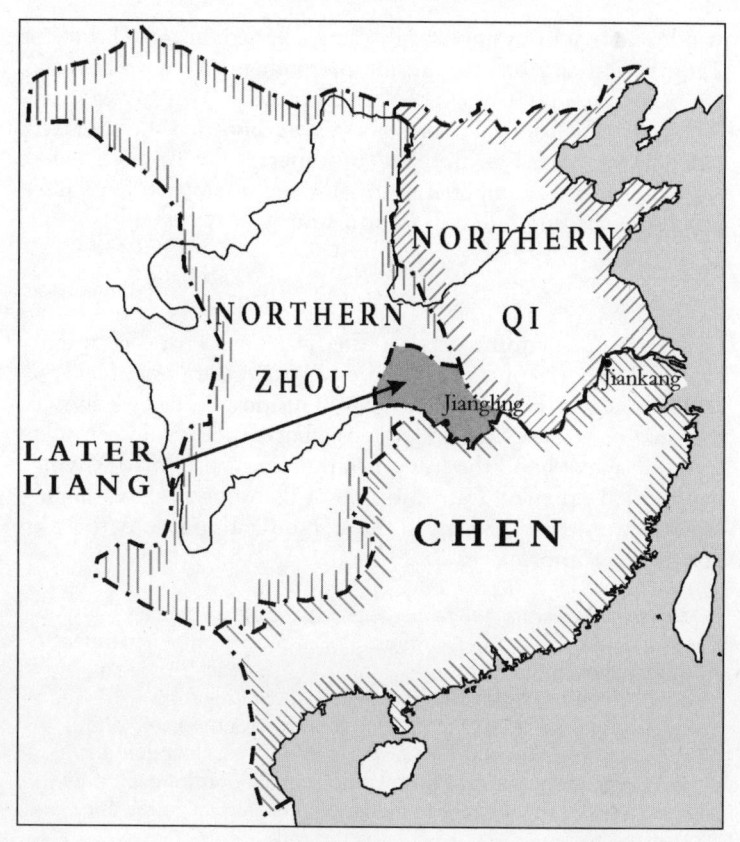

Three Kingdoms in 560

group of specialized histories of the Northern and Southern Dynasties, all written in the standard 'annals/biography' form by officials in the Bureau of History. But remarkably, within a couple of generations, various private historians had produced alternative histories of the same period, using the time-honoured 'chronology' framework[2]. All were lost during the Song period, but one of them is our target here today.

The point has already been made that a project like this aims at more than just recovering bits of text. Among other things it will look for serious new insights into Chinese history. From the Tang period and before, outside the standard dynastic histories, we have very few surviving historical records. To recover something like this from the hand of a private historian should give a rare chance to get behind the bureaucratically inspired values and choices of the imperial historians, and discover other values, other choices, and different information.

☆

In the reconstruction workshop the first tool to hand is an entry from the imperial library catalogue of 1042 – the *General catalogue [of the Court] in Honour of Literature*. This now lost work showed the state of the imperial collections after decades had been spent trying to make good the losses from the great fire in 1015 which had burned down all four institutes of the Song imperial library. The relevant entry (preserved through quotation in other works) gives a most informative description:

> *Summary documents of three kingdoms* – 30 scroll/chapters – composed by Qiu Yue, administrator in the revenue department of Fen zhou [prefecture] under the Tang. It treats [the regions of] Guanzhong, Yedu, and Jiangnan as three kingdoms. Beginning with the Western Wei, it ends with the Later Zhou, encompassing Wei and Northern Qi in the east, including Liang and Chen in the south. Thirty sections in all, but there are now many gaps in the sequence of chapters: chapters 21 to the end are missing.[3]

These few lines sketch out a basic ground plan for the whole project. Notice first of all that the cataloguers were working with an actual copy of the book, not just reproducing an entry in some other bibliography. Although the copy they described in 1042 was obviously defective, lacking 10 out of its 30 chapters, they were still in a position to pass on information which must have stood clearly at the head of the text: the book's scale, its author's name and appointment, its chronological character, and its actual chronological scope. It's very tempting to read the remarks about the three kingdoms and the overall time-plan as reflecting phrases from the author's own original preface, now lost.

There is a little information about this author, but not much, in the two versions of the *History of the Tang*.[4] When we boil down what comes out of the various references there, the picture emerges of a man who reached the very highest levels of scholarly dignity in the Tang establishment. He served on the academic staff of the future emperor Rui zong between 707 and 710,[5] was tutor to his son the royal prince Li Fan between 710 and 712,[6] and became a member of one of the colleges of academics who directly advised the emperor on intellectual, documentary, and ritual matters, as well as teaching selected students. He died in 715 or soon after, in the early reign of Xuan zong (712–756).[7] Which makes it all the more interesting that his position recorded with the authorship of *Summary documents* (no doubt as it appeared in the text itself) was a much humbler provincial post. Sadly we know too little about his career to learn more from that detail – for instance, exactly when in his life he completed this book.

The book's title makes a series of appearances in imperial bibliographies of the Song period. It was still in the imperial collections in the twelfth century, according to the catalogue of 1178, but vanishes from the record after the Song.[8] So the time has come to turn from the ground plan to the actual remains.

Those remains can be found in half-a-dozen textual sources, two of which are particularly important. One is the *Imperial reader* completed by 984. It has become fashionable to say that this famous source included only material copied from older encyclopedias existing before the mid-seventh century.[9] But in the last lecture I pointed out that scores of works from the Tang period are represented there, from the seventh, eighth, ninth and tenth centuries, almost up to the date when the *Imperial reader* itself was compiled. Our text was one of them: about 300 quotations from it appear in this source. So the first task is to gather the quotations, transcribe and edit them, and link them as far as possible to the known historical record.

Remember, this work was a chronology, which makes the second main source particularly crucial – Sima Guang's general chronology of Chinese history, the *Full exemplary guide for use in government*, compiled between 1066 and 1084.[10] That great historian used our text as one of his main sources for the years beginning 534. We know this because he often points it out in his own critical notes on matters of dating and variant details of recorded events.[11] Nearly a hundred such citations lie scattered through the chronology of the mid-sixth century. These notes give a much more detailed shape to the ground plan of the *Summary documents of three kingdoms*. They are still, of course, just occasional glints of light which confirm that Sima Guang was using this source, because he only actually mentions a source when he has some choice to make or problem to discuss. Most of the time he uses his sources in silence, and we have reason to assume that good chunks of historical narrative in his great chronology were actually adapted from Qiu Yue's book *Summary documents* – it's just that we can't identify them all. So the ground plan is visible to us, but very little of the detail.

The fullest picture we can draw from all this comes by assigning dates to the many bits of text from the *Imperial reader*, then bringing them together with the structure of the chronology *Full exemplary guide* – one might say adding flesh to the bones. Something interesting then appears. The *Full exemplary guide* first mentions our text under the year 534, which was the year of the split of the Eastern from the Western Wei. No problem there: the imperial catalogue of 1042 already makes clear that this year was indeed the starting point of Qiu Yue's book. But its *last* mention of *Summary documents* comes under the year 563, in other words nearly twenty years before the end of the Northern/Southern Dynasties period. After that, complete silence.

The explanation appears when we look again at the catalogue of 1042. The last ten chapters, or one third of the *Summary documents*, had been lost by that date, and it seems clear (from those twenty years of silence) that Sima Guang was using a similarly defective copy in the 1070s. But the compilers of the *Imperial reader* were not: they quote text for events which happened all through until the early years of the Sui dynasty in the 580s. They either had a full copy of the text to use, or they were recycling quotations from someone else who did. It is a reminder of the unique importance of that source, speaking as it does for library holdings at the very start of the Song period.

Let's look again at a line in the catalogue entry of 1042: 'Beginning with the Western Wei, it ends with the Later Zhou, encompassing Wei and Northern Qi in the east, including Liang and Chen in the south.' The *Summary documents of three kingdoms* was a chronology, structured on a year-by-year, month-by-month, day-by-day sequence, and a scheme like that obviously needs to follow a governing system of dates. Working with a unified imperial dynasty makes this easy, because the reign periods are standard and universal. But dealing with a divided China forces the historian to make choices – whose dates is he going to follow? Here we have the answer: Qiu Yue follows the sequence of Western Wei to Northern Zhou.[12] All the other kingdoms are secondary to those.

It's an interesting decision, and its effect leaps out from the page when we actually read the text of *Summary documents*. The rulers of Western Wei and Northern Zhou are referred to by their own imperial titles; but the rulers of Liang, Chen and Qi are nearly always labelled as 'Masters' (*zhu*) of their kingdoms. And much more striking is a phrase we read several times when the Zhou are fighting their enemies: Qiu Yue writes 'our army' (*wo jun*) or 'our troops' (*wo bing*) to refer to the Zhou.[13] Remember that the Northern Zhou rulers were not Han Chinese, while their enemies the Liang and Chen in the south were. Qiu Yue himself came from a Han Chinese family,[14] yet he identifies here with the Tuoba and Xianbei dynasties.

We should not regard that as some kind of ethnic treason: Qiu Yue made his decision for reasons to do with the succession of power. His own imperial masters, the Tang, had received power from the Sui, who received it from the Northern Zhou, who received it from the Western Wei. Each of those transmissions of power is recorded as a public ritual act in the standard histories.[15] To privilege the sequence from Western Wei to Zhou reflects a Tang notion of imperial legitimacy which made all the other kingdoms illegitimate and peripheral. Ethnicity seems to have nothing to do with it.

Yet during the Northern Song dynasty those values changed. Sima Guang in the 1070s mapped his chronology of the Northern/Southern Dynasties period upon the Han Chinese-ruled dynasties of the south – a decision which speaks for a different notion of legitimacy, in which the northern kingdoms under other ethnic groups become peripheral.[16] It's one more sign of the gathering strength of national consciousness, closely associated with the Han people, which we know set in with the Song dynasty and has reached its most intense expression in the nationalism of the twentieth century. Qiu Yue reminds us that China was not always like that. And he can do this because, unlike the authors of individual dynastic histories of the same period a generation before him, he has had to choose where overall legitimacy lay in a period of division.

I find three levels of significance in this catalogue entry. The first is straightforwardly editorial – it informs us simply how Qiu Yue defined his period for purposes of chronology, and helps his modern editors to know what dates to place at the head of each year's entries. The second level distinguishes Qiu Yue in the eighth century from Sima Guang in the eleventh: it reveals how the two historians differed in their priorities and conceptions of legitimacy. But the most general and powerful significance is this: the concept of China as a sovereign state under Han ethnic rulers, striving to resist the usurping rule of alien peoples, is not a permanent, immutable quantity. It has not always been in place. It emerged and grew as part of the new cast of thought and the transformed Chinese world that came with the transition from Tang to Song.

☆

The practical tasks of reconstruction bring interesting problems into view. To work on a chronology with a clear master plan of dates does give a huge advantage over most of the reconstructive work done through recent centuries by Chinese scholars: their editions of lost early works were often condemned to remain a random heap of gathered quotations with no informing structure. With the *Summary documents of three kingdoms*, once dates can be assigned to the quotations, they fall naturally into their place in the overall scheme, not least when the *Full exemplary guide for use in government* identifies the month and day for us. A certain number of quotations obligingly supply their own date. The majority of the rest can be dated by cross-reference to the standard dynastic histories for the period. (And it is an enormous help to have available a digital database of that corpus, which quickly ferrets out passages in unpredictable places.)

Yet problems do remain to be solved or acknowledged. Numbers of quotations in the *Imperial reader* and elsewhere are drawn from what are quite clearly biographical notices of historical figures: they give assessments of character, anecdotes from childhood, personal incidents of no general historical significance. How did that material fit into the chronological history of events? Editors of a reconstruction must find a solution to questions like this, and in practice the answer comes here by studying one of the very few chronological works actually transmitted from the Tang, the *Veritable record of Jiankang*, compiled by Xu Song in 756. This was a history of the southern dynasties, with their capital at Jiankang, from 222 to 589. Xu Song dealt with the problem of biographical data within a chronological format by inserting each individual's biographical notice retrospectively at the time of his death.[17] That has seemed a rational and practical system to follow in restoring the *Summary documents*.

It still, however, leaves open a more serious underlying question. No matter how much circumstantial evidence is there to guide an editor in reconstructing a lost book from quotations, there must come a point at which conjecture and hypothesis take over in shaping the result. What finally emerges from the work of reconstruction is a new artifact with its own characteristics, formed as much by the thought-processes of the restorer as by the residual textual legacy from the past. The point comes home most sharply when we survey the end product of assembling so many quotations within the known chronological structure. It then becomes clear how little actually survives. From the original book with its thirty chapters the work of reconstruction has retrieved only about 19 to 20 thousand characters, perhaps a tenth of the whole text. Fixed in their place, the fragments of quotation suggest nothing more than recovered sweepings from some object smashed into thousands of small pieces. Broken off from their surrounding context, what significance can they bring with them, by comparison with the lost original text?

Needless to say the even more fundamental problems of textual transmission underlie the whole enterprise. *Summary documents of three kingdoms* was already approaching 300 years old when the early Song compilers did their work on it: unknown generations of copyists had already left their mark on the text by then. But the act of quotation in compilations like the *Imperial reader* and the *Extensive records* represents a far more open and chancy episode in textual survival. And the transmission of those two compilations themselves through the past thousand years has in turn been fraught with loss and risk. Modern editors have a duty to acknowledge these dangers and deal with them by the use of text-critical apparatus. Here again their product takes on the look of a modern artifact.

☆

Acknowledging dangers does not mean surrendering to despair. The historical value of the project emerges from the distinctiveness of the recovered text. And this shows up most strongly in the narrative of great events, to which we now turn. 'Spectacular, tragic and appalling' was how I described the period just now, and the description best fits the events surrounding the fall of the Liang dynasty in the south. Let us remember first that a violent rebellion under Hou Jing had brought the long reign of emperor Wu to an end by penetrating the royal palace at Jiankang in 548, and installing a puppet emperor. Hou Jing himself was put down in the summer of 552, and on December 13 in that year the throne of Liang passed to the emperor Yuan.

At the time of his accession this man was in the city of Jiangling on the middle Yangzi. The capital city Jiankang and the surrounding regions were devastated, and an important policy decision soon faced the new emperor: should he move back to the original capital, or remain in Jiangling and make a new capital there? At first he was inclined to go back to Jiankang. But a strongly argued debate started up in court. One side argued against going back to Jiankang – it was finished as a royal capital, they said; the northern enemies were only just across the river, leaving the place vulnerable in an emergency; whereas Jiangling was an ideal site for a new emperor to emerge. Against this a pro-Jiankang lobby argued that the people would not accept emperor Yuan as a legitimate ruler unless they saw him take his throne in the ancient capital. The two sides in this debate accused each other of pursuing their own local interests. The emperor, we read, laughed and called for a vote to be held: an assembly of 500 civil and military officials voted by a show of hands, and the majority was for going back to Jiankang. One of them, called Zhu Maichen, came forward to reinforce the message and urge the emperor to decide accordingly (he stressed that he was arguing against his own local interest).

Down to this point we can piece together the details of the scene in court, rather clumsily, from different passages scattered around in the standard histories, mostly in the biographies of individuals who made speeches during the debate. But something strange now follows. Emperor Yuan did not return to Jiankang, but set up his capital in Jiangling. Why did he decide to do that? The standard histories are silent on the matter. (Even Xu Song, in his *Veritable records of Jiankang*, left it out.)[18] But in *Summary documents of three kingdoms* we have a full narrative account of the whole episode, and there we read that after hearing the debate, holding the vote, and receiving Zhu Maichen's final comment, the emperor called in a diviner called Du Jinghao to clinch the matter. The divination came out unfavourably, and the message was "Don't go". Even the diviner was embarrassed by this. He said: "This omen was left by some bandit demon."[19] But still, against all the weight of opinion and perhaps against his own inclinations, the emperor decided to stay. The rest, as they say, is history. After taking that decision in the summer of 553, emperor Yuan was on the throne for little more than a year before an army of the Western Wei invaded his capital (early in 555) and took his life. The Liang became a small client state, still based at Jiangling, within the borders of Western Wei and later of Northern Zhou.

This whole episode will stand a lot of analysis. The ultimate source for these events in the Liang court was no doubt the diary of court proceedings kept through every emperor's reign (the *Qi ju zhu*), followed by later derivatives. But the early Tang historians made their own choices on how to use that material, what to include, what to exclude. The value of Qiu Yue's work is that it gives us information left out of the standard histories. I find it significant, once again, on three levels. The first, most simply, is that it fills in a gap in our information: we now know why the Liang emperor Yuan decided to make Jiangling his new capital city. But there is a second, much larger issue here. By any standards this was a major policy decision. The siting of a capital was an important ritual act in medieval China, but also a serious strategic commitment. If Jiankang had been restored as the Liang capital, the dynasty would have stood in a quite different strategic position in relation to the rival kingdoms in the north. The nearest potential enemy would have been the Northern Qi, not the Western Wei – quite possibly a weaker opponent which would have allowed the Liang to survive unchallenged for longer. In any case the balance of power would have looked different. Yet emperor Yuan took this solemn decision, against the best available advice, on the basis of an act of divination which even the diviner mistrusted. On the toss of a coin, we might say. So Qiu Yue's information has serious implications for how we view the events of the mid-sixth century.

There is a still more important dimension to all this – the silence of the imperial historians on the matter. Why did they leave the crucial stage of the policy decision out of the official record? It was, of course, an action familiar to Chinese historians ever since the birth of chronological history in the canonical *Spring and autumn annals*: the so-called '*Spring and autumn* brush' was used to imply moral comments by the historian through the indirect manipulation and selection of material for recording. We can suppose that the early Tang imperial historians meant their silence to express condemnation of an irrational act. They were, after all, bureaucrats writing history for other bureaucrats to read:[20] the business of court affairs was in their view a matter for systematic advice and control by the bureaucracy. They were always uncomfortable with divination. Books on divination were one of the categories quite badly under-represented in their official bibliographies. So interventions by the likes of diviners, who clearly represented an intrusion into decision-making beyond the reach of bureaucratic control, were not welcome. But Qiu Yue wrote his chronology in a private capacity, in a different spirit: he felt free to transcribe his sources more fully, bring more facts to the surface. And he was encumbered with no sense of loyalty towards the Liang dynasty.

If the standard histories of the Northern/Southern Dynasties kept silence on emperor Yuan's decision about Jiankang, how many more serious policy decisions did they leave underreported or even misreported in the same way? And if they did it for this period, what about the rest of imperial history? To these big questions Qiu Yue gives us tempting, though still rather limited clues.

Let me offer you another important example: the matter of burning books. We have seen that part of the downside of imperial China's interest in centralizing the books of the whole world was their physical vulnerability. Rare and important books were systematically collected and assembled in wooden library structures, where they were fatally open to destruction by war and fire. Destruction of libraries by fire happened many times in Chinese history, inflicting terrible damage and loss on the written heritage. But the Liang dynasty saw this happen twice within six years. And both times there is the horrible suspicion that it was the result of conscious acts.

When the rebel Hou Jing penetrated the imperial compound in 548, he found hundreds of courtesans in the eastern palace and entertained his officers to a huge party there. A fire broke out, everyone fled, and hundreds of cabinets of books in the eastern palace were burned up. This brought to pass a dream warning given to the Crown Prince, the future emperor Jianwen: in the dream a man had painted a figure of the First Qin Emperor, saying, "This man wants to burn the books again!" According to one of the dynastic histories it was the

Crown Prince himself who ordered this fire to be set. But Qiu Yue's account does not allege that: he simply reports the dream and the fire.[21]

In all events, a large proportion of the Liang dynasty's magnificent collection of rare books was destroyed, and the remnants of the collection went to the new capital at Jiangling. There, in 555, the palace was exposed to another invading army. As the Western Wei troops closed in on the palace, the Liang ruler, we read,

> realized that things were beyond rescue, went to the Bamboo Hall of the Eastern Building, and ordered his secretary Gao Shanbao to burn 140,000 scrolls of books and charts ancient and modern. He wanted to throw himself into the flames and perish with them, but his palace staff pulled at his robes. Then, once the fire had burned everything up, he hacked at a pillar with his jewelled swords so that they were smashed, exclaiming: "Civil and military culture comes to its end this night!"[22]

The words of this account found their way, little changed, into the *Full exemplary guide*, and it is very tempting to assume that Sima Guang is transcribing from our text, *Summary documents*, both here and when he reports that a few days later emperor Yuan was asked why he had burned his books and smashed his precious swords. The emperor apparently said: "I had read ten thousand scrolls of books, and yet this day still came to pass. That's why I burned them." For him, of course, it *was* the end of the road: he wanted the books to perish with him.

Now this event stands out as important both in actual and in symbolic terms. The loss of the Liang library cut off from transmission a significant number of Chinese books, many of which we can see named and detailed in the bibliographical chapters of the Sui dynastic history. According to the late Tang art critic Zhang Yanyuan, quantities of painting and calligraphy perished too. This was, quite simply, one of the historic disasters of Chinese civilization. But for it to be inflicted consciously and deliberately by an emperor, the trustee of that civilization in transmission and himself a writer of some importance – that is a disaster of another dimension.

Yet the dynastic histories fail to give us all the facts alleged in this narrative.[23] And they cover the tracks so successfully that a modern scholar, the Dutch historian Erik Zürcher, has argued in these terms:

> The pathetic and probably apocryphal story of the Liang emperor Yüan burning his own collection is not endorsed by *Liang-shu* 5.29a–b, which only speaks of a conflagration coinciding with a violent storm, and not of any intentional destruction.[24]

I disagree with this verdict on the story. But why? Why not accept a more sceptical view of the tragedy, in harmony with the dynastic histories, and dismiss Qiu Yue's version as sensation-peddling? For me the really important reason why not is not so much the willingness of such men as Zhang Yanyuan and Sima Guang to endorse Qiu Yue's version (which they did), as the very nature of the silence in the dynastic histories. The *History of the Liang* cited by Zürcher manages to conceal not just the role of emperor Yuan, but even the burning of the imperial library as such. Yes, it does mention a fire in the capital city, but no more than that. Arguably the destruction of the Liang dynasty's library was the ultimate, conclusive act in its own downfall. Would that not deserve a mention in the official history? But there was evidently something so sinister about the event that silence seemed more important to the historians than telling the facts as they knew them. That sinister element is what Qiu Yue reveals in his version of events: it provides an adequate explanation for what we would now call an act of censorship by the official historians.

It all reminds me of the doctoring of official photographs in the political annals of the twentieth century. Everyone here has seen those side-by-side versions of identical photographs with smiling individuals in view on one side, but vanished on the other. What we should remember about this, perhaps, is that the political class among whom those photographs and events were significant carried a fuller knowledge of them than the official record revealed. The silence and the invisibility were significant in themselves: they were inherently political statements and were surely recognized as such. I am prepared to believe that in seventh-century China, too, the recorded circumstances of the Liang emperor Yuan's fire were widely known among the official class, but they would also have understood why, in the official record, those full circumstances should be conspicuous by their absence.

It is interesting to contrast Qiu Yue's treatment of the fire of 555 in Jiangling with the way he treated the fire of 548 in Jiankang: we noted that he seems not to have held the Crown Prince openly accountable for that disaster. I feel insecure in arguing about material we don't find in the remains of *Summary documents*: we are after all not reading an original text, only a patchwork of quotations, possibly even second-hand quotations, which maybe suffered damage on their way through to us. But it seems to me useful to point out the difference that separates those two great fires. The first, in Jiankang, was an act of war targeted against a rebel who had invaded the royal palace: even if the fire went out of control and destroyed books, the fundamental motivation was last-ditch defence. But the fire in Jiangling was a self-destructive act of nihilistic despair. With the hindsight of the Tang dynasty, this would have seemed a significant distinction, and one which deserved to go on the record. We can at least guess why Qiu Yue took different decisions about recording these events than the men of the Bureau of History a generation before him.

Great events have taken up a big part of this lecture: I hope the insights that come out of them have justified it. But of course there is more to history than single great events, and we ought not to leave the *Summary documents of three kingdoms* without asking what special feel it might give for the texture and quality of life at large in those dangerous times.

It would be wise not to entertain too many lavish expectations. Quite a large proportion of the recovered text is very similar indeed to passages in the dynastic histories. Matching every possible sentence systematically with the official record has made it clear that Qiu Yue was working from essentially the same sources. But even so his work reveals many small details which have not otherwise been transmitted – that is, material left out of the standard record which Qiu Yue nonetheless decided to include. What does that material tell us? Overwhelmingly it conveys a much richer picture of the role of omens, divination, spirit-mediums and local religious cults in the lives of the social elite. Here are some examples . . .

The Northern Qi dignitary Cui Jishu would meet his end in 573, in an interesting episode of inter-ethnic suspicion and mistrust.[25] But first came a series of omens in his domestic life. He found that the flower stems in his lotus pool at home all turned into the heads of warriors wearing so-called Xianbei hats (the Xianbei, of course, were the rulers of Northern Zhou, who would soon conquer the Northern Qi).[26] Then Cui's wife had a daytime dream or vision of a large hairy monster coming up menacingly close to her, they consulted a spirit medium (*wu*), and were told that this was the General of the Five Paths (Wudao Dajiang), whose appearance in a private home was an omen of misfortune.[27] Then a large white object descended from the sky to a point a few inches above the head of Cui's son, before vanishing; then a huge arm, ten feet long, sprouted out from the ground in his main hall at home, brilliantly lighting the interior; but no one else could see it.[28]

Here is another type of record. During the year 567, there was in Wu'an (now in Hebei, then in the kingdom of Northern Qi) a cult leader whose followers claimed that they had been cured of blindness and lameness by drinking from a spring in which a Golden Buddha was found. An enormous following built up around this. What was eventually found there was a yellow toad, looking like gold all over, which moved in and out of the water. But everyone, from the Qi emperor Wucheng and his courtiers down, drank from the waters of the spring.[29]

For the official dynastic historians all this kind of thing was presumably tittle-tattle, casual, anecdotal stuff that would rarely earn a place in the national records. For us it is, first, a glimpse into the mental world of the sixth century. It is also a sign that other kinds of historical vision were possible in Tang China when a private historian turned his hand to writing the history of that period. It reveals to us wider horizons of perception concerning the lives, actions and destinies of people in the past: not only did the men and women of the sixth century attend to omens at key points in their lives, and patronize healing cults, but these things were significant to a historian writing about their times a century and a half later.

History is something constructed by historians. For the Northern and Southern Dynasties the historians of our own time are busy with late-twentieth century constructions which reflect the state of knowledge, but also of course the priorities and fashions of our own time and culture. We do need the dynastic histories transmitted to us by the Chinese imperial system because, particularly for this relatively early period, they preserve nearly all the detailed narrative documentation we can find. We have a sharp and well-developed perception of the limitations of those histories, and it is customary to epitomize them (as just now) as constructions by imperial bureaucrats for the use of imperial bureaucrats. In spite of this, I believe that the dynastic histories *can* yield a much more rounded picture of those earlier periods from than first impressions suggest. But what the *Summary documents of three kingdoms* provides is the luxury of another kind of source. History becomes most interesting when the sources don't fit well together, don't like one another, set up tensions among themselves. We are then forced at every point to recognize the contingency of any particular record, to see it in a context, to look for its motivation. Even though Qiu Yue drew on the same documentary materials as the Bureau of History, he approached his task differently, and the tensions show through in many small ways. I believe we can learn useful things from them.

Bibliographers, I hope, will find another kind of value here. Aside from the sheer antiquarian pleasure of restoring a lost item from the past, we can contemplate a text which transmission has failed to preserve, and seek out the reasons why. My basic argument has been that certain books fail to keep their appeal into later times, and the *Summary documents*, with its characteristically Tang view of imperial legitimacy, met this fate. The imperial state created and maintained its own historical records. From Song times on, the Han-ruled dynasties of the south, not the alien dynasties of the north, were perceived to carry dynastic legitimacy. So this old, eighth-century work will have seemed remote and unintelligible in its historical focus. Nor will its raw historical narrative have raised much interest once so much of it had been incorporated by Sima Guang into the grand panorama of his *Full exemplary guide for use in government*. With a standard chronological narrative to serve as permanent authority, what need of that outdated and historically circumscribed work any more? The *Summary documents* was simply buried by time, and its distinctive early Tang vision of the last fifty years of disunion vanished with it.

NOTES

1 The labours and discoveries of this research were shared with me by Zhao Chao 趙超, a scholar from the Institute of Archaeology, Chinese Academy of Social Sciences. Our project received support from the British Academy, the K. C. Wong Foundation, and the University of Oxford. The resulting critical edition appeared in Chinese as Du Deqiao 杜德橋 and Zhao Chao 趙超, eds., *Sanguo dian lüe ji jiao* 三國典略輯校, Taibei 1998. Earlier lectures on this topic were given at the University of Durham, the University of California at Berkeley, and Pomona College.

2 See Denis Twitchett, *The writing of official history under the T'ang*, Cambridge 1992, p. 64, with note 4.

3 Quoted in *Wenxian tong kao* 文獻通考, Zhejiang shuju edn., 1896, 195.19a, and also, in abridged and slightly variant form, in *Yu hai* 47.10b. In 1781 this passage was transcribed into the summary catalogue *Chongwen zong mu* 3.7b by the editors of *Siku quan shu* 四庫全書. A critical account of the lost full text of *Chongwen zong mu* and its fragmentary remains is given by Piet van der Loon, *Taoist books in the libraries of the Sung period: a critical study and index*, London 1984, pp. 6–8.

4 There are biographies of Qiu Yue 丘悅 in *Jiu Tang shu* 190B.5015; *Xin Tang shu* 新唐書, Beijing 1975, 112.4163. See also references in *Jiu Tang shu* 98.3079–80; *Xin Tang shu* 127.4452, and 112.4162.

5 *Jiu Tang shu* dates this to the period Jinglong 景龍, 707–710.

6 *Jiu Tang shu* and *Xin Tang shu* both use the title Prince of Qi 岐王, a title conferred on Li Fan 李範 when his father came to

the throne as Rui zong 睿宗, which dates Qiu's appointment to 710–712.

7 More detailed discussion of biographical data, including the Qiu family's place of origin in Wuxing 吳興 and Qiu Yue's position in the Zhaowen guan 昭文館 college, appears in Du and Zhao, *Sanguo dian lüe ji jiao*, '*Sanguo dian lüe* gailun' 《三國典略》概論, pp. 1–3.

8 *Zhongxing guan ge shu mu* 中興館閣書目, ap. *Yu hai* 47.10ab, translated below in note 12. The now lost catalogue was completed in 1178 and represented the state of the imperial collections as recovered since the fall of the northern capital Kaifeng in 1127. Note that a summary entry, with author, title and number of chapters (20), appears in the bibliographical monograph of *Song shi* 203.5088, compiled in 1345 from catalogues of Song date. In the case of this entry the *Song shi* no doubt derived its information from *Zhongxing si chao guo shi* 中興四朝國史 (1257, now lost), where the bibliographical monograph in turn derived it from *Zhongxing guan ge shu mu*. These relationships are explained and documented by Piet van der Loon, *Taoist books in the libraries of the Sung period*, pp. 17–20.

9 See note 45 to Lecture I.

10 The section dealing with the mid-sixth century, under the Liang 梁 and Chen 陳 dynasties, was done between 1071 and 1076: see Cao Jiaqi 曹家琪, '*Zi zhi tong jian* bianxiu kao' 資治通鑒編修考, *Wen shi* 文史 5, Beijing 1978, p. 82.

11 Sima Guang's 司馬光 procedures are described by E. G. Pulleyblank, 'Chinese historical criticism: Liu Chih-chi and Ssu-ma Kuang', in W. G. Beasley and E. G. Pulleyblank, eds., *Historians of China and Japan*, London 1961, pp. 135–66, with pp. 151–9.

12 The *Zhongxing guan ge shu mu* referred more explicitly to the chronology of *Sanguo dian lüe*. It reads: 'From the time when the Wei of the Yuan [family] 元魏 split into Eastern and Western, the Western Wei 西魏 made its capital in Guanzhong 關中, and the Later Zhou 後周 succeeded it; the Eastern Wei 東魏 made its capital in Ye 鄴, and the Northern Qi 北齊 succeeded it; the Liang 梁 and Chen 陳 both made their capital in Jiangnan 江南. [Qiu] Yue's book is headed with the opening of the Western Wei, though it narrates of Yuwen Tai 宇文泰': see quotation in *Yu hai* 47.10b. Yuwen Tai (507–556) held the title Counsellor-in-Chief (*chengxiang* 丞相) of the Western Wei from its foundation, wielded full power throughout that kingdom's life, and died at the point when his own family assumed dynastic power as the Later Zhou. In that sense the sequence Western Wei to Northern Zhou covers the full span of the Yuwen cycle of power.

13 For examples of this see *Taiping yu lan*, Song edn. repr. Beijing 1960, 304.3b, 313.3a, 323.8b, 326.1b.

14 On this point see above, note 7.

15 *Bei shi*, Beijing 1974, 9.331; *Sui shu* 1.11–13; *Sui shu* 5.102.

16 The legitimacy of the Northern or the Southern Dynasties was closely studied and sharply debated during the Northern Song period. Sima Guang's statement (in *Zi zhi tong jian*, repr. Beijing 1956, 69.2185–8) stresses the need for a single overall scheme of dates without presuming to enter judgement on individual regimes. Yet he 'has no alternative' but to follow the transmission of dynastic power from Jin to Song, to Qi, to Liang, to Chen, and thus to Sui and Tang (69.2187–8), and this was endorsed in later times. I am grateful to Dr Joachim Mittag for a discussion of the question.

17 But this format is maintained only for the first ten of the work's twenty chapters. The rest revert to a standard annals/biography format, dynasty by dynasty. On this point see the modern reprint edition by Zhang Chenshi 張忱石: *Jiankang shi lu* 建康實錄, Beijing 1986, editorial preface, pp. 25–6.

18 The relevant passages from *Zhou shu* 周書, Beijing 1971, 41.730, *Nan shi* 南史, Beijing 1975, 8.244 and 34.899–900, *Chen shu* 陳書, Beijing 1972, 24.309, and *Jiankang shi lu* 20.787 are assembled in Du and Zhao, *Sanguo dian lüe ji jiao*, pp. 86–7.

19 *Taiping yu lan* 156.4b–5a, and 726.2b (a second quotation from the same passage).

20 This much-cited formulation was first proposed by Etienne Balazs in 'L'histoire comme guide de la pratique bureaucratique (les monographies, les encyclopédies, les recueils de statuts)', in Beasley and Pulleyblank, *Historians of China and Japan*, p. 82: 'l'histoire est écrite *par des fonctionnaires pour des fonctionnaires*.'

21 Compare *Nan shi* 80.1999–2000 with *Sanguo dian lüe*, ap. *Taiping yu lan* 619.7a.

22 *Taiping yu lan* 619.7a, citing *Sanguo dianlüe*. The phrase 'civil and military culture' paraphrases the Chinese *wen wu zhi dao* 文武之道. That phrase could also be construed with reference to Confucius and his appeal to 'the way of Kings Wen and Wu [of the Zhou]': *Lun yu* 19/22.

23 The relevant passages in *Nan shi* 8.244–5, *Liang shu*, Beijing 1973, 5.135, and *Zi zhi tong jian* 165.5121–2, are transcribed in Du and Zhao, *Sanguo dian lüe ji jiao*, p.101.

24 Erik Zürcher, 'Recent studies on Chinese painting', *T'oung Pao* 51, 1964, p. 415.

25 See *Bei Qi shu*, Beijing 1972, 8.107, and *Zi zhi tong jian* 171.5328; biographies of Cui Jishu 崔季舒 in *Wei shu*, Beijing 1974, 57.1273, and *Bei Qi shu* 39.511–3.
26 On the Xianbei hat see Lü Yifei 呂一飛, 'Xianbei mao 鮮卑帽', *Wen shi* 30, Beijing 1988, p. 82.
27 On Wudao Dajiang 五道大將 see Glen Dudbridge, 'The General of the Five Paths in Tang and pre-Tang China', *Cahiers d'Extrême-Asie* 9, 1996–1997, 85–98. This deity, of Indian Buddhist origin, lived on in China as a martial figure keeping guard at the frontier of the other world and supervising the transition of the newly dead.
28 *Taiping yu lan* 734.9b, 975.6a; *Taiping guang ji* 361.2862. Although the latter two passages are ascribed to different sources (*Bei Qi shu* and *Bei shi*), they do not actually appear in those transmitted works and quite probably come from *Sanguo dianlüe*, like the first.
29 *Taiping yu lan* 949.3a.

III

Classification: the case of
The Four Gentlemen of Liang

LET ME BEGIN BY RECALLING a claim made by Zheng Qiao in the twelfth century: 'If books perish it is because their classification is not distinct; if the classification were distinct, then the many schools and traditions of learning would each have their ordered principle and, even when [seemingly] lost, would not be able to perish'.[1] The book discussed in my last lecture, *Summary documents of three kingdoms*, seems to falsify that claim. Although its known appearances in classified catalogues and bibliographies show no sign of ambiguity in its status as a work of chronological history,[2] it still failed to survive. Yet those catalogue entries did provide essential tools in the task of reconstructing the lost work and giving it shape. The example confirms what all students of Chinese bibliography know well, that the catalogues of imperial, and later of private, libraries, bequeathing data which cast such a sharp light on the books of China over two millennia, are one of the glories of its book culture.

Subject classification, as we found in the first lecture, was an inherent part of that culture. But with it came not necessarily clarity so much as the grip of a centrally imposed scheme of values. I have argued that the survival or loss of books had more to do with value systems than with clarity of category. This lecture, with the help of a second example, will aim to go further, to test the very adequacy of traditional classifications to match or control the richness of the literature they sought to describe.

☆

The Four Gentlemen of Liang, also a book of the eighth century, presents a different case from *Summary records of three kingdoms*. It was short, and we probably have a far more healthy proportion of its original text. It is a book about which the known facts have been collected and are on the record. Yet to my view it remains a more mysterious piece of work than *Summary records*. If we ask precisely what kind of book this was, what conclusion or point it was leading up to, how it might relate to other works in Chinese literature, the answers seem strangely elusive. I shall argue that this failure of clarity is not a matter for disappointment, but a cause for satisfaction: it suggests that by recovering what we can of the book we are adding something new and interesting to the store of Chinese literature.

Modern Chinese scholars and critics are serenely untroubled by any sense of failure over this text. They have published excellent investigative research on what remains of it, and for them it fits neatly into ready-made, but modern, categories. Some of their judgements will come up for discussion later. Put simply, it seems hard to believe that these critics are reading the same text as the one that presents itself to me. That is what will need discussion.

The most sharply focused external information available from someone who actually owned a copy of *The Four Gentlemen of Liang* comes in Chen Zhensun's catalogue of his private collection. This was completed after 1240, which shows that a version of *The Four Gentlemen* was there in the mid-thirteenth century. The work had survived for at least five hundred years.[3]

Let me summarize the catalogue entry.[4] The book consists of just one scroll/chapter. It is ascribed to Zhang Yue (667–731), a statesman and important poet and prose writer of the early eighth century.[5] Chen consults progressively earlier catalogues for information on authorship, but gets varied and confusing results. The 1178 descriptive catalogue of the Southern Song imperial library[6] said it was compiled by Liang Zaiyan; the *New history of the Tang* bibliography (1060) had Lu Shen, but noted a variant ascription to Liang Zaiyan;[7] a private catalogue of 1049[8] said that Liang Zaiyan gained his material from someone called Tian Tong of Linzi, but also noted that other versions were credited with the names of Zhang Yue or Lu Shen. Chen finds the evidence of the book itself confusing: at the end it does report matters concerning Tian Tong, yet it is still headed with the name of Zhang Yue. This is somehow consistent with the early catalogue evidence, but not really clear – to him or to me. In any case, Chen Zhensun finds the things recorded in this book, which he classifies under 'Transmitted Records' within the 'Histories' category, too wild and extravagant to be worth much scrutiny. And he notices that the Four Gentlemen of Liang had funny names. So much comes out of the bibliographical resources available in the thirteenth century.

What now remains of this book is chiefly three solid slabs of text in *Extensive records for the time of Supreme Peace*. Call them A, B and C.[9] At first sight they should represent a good part of the textual material in the book held in Tai zong's library. The reason for saying so is that the *Imperial reader for the time of Supreme Peace* gives eight quotations from the same book: all of these match passages in A, B or C from the *Extensive records*, but they seem a little better in textual quality, which suggests that the *Imperial reader* compilers did their work independently of the *Extensive records* (completed at least four years earlier in 978), and used the source-book directly. The fact that their eight quotations nonetheless still fall within the material covered by *Extensive records* makes it seem that there was not much of the text left unquoted there.

But that is not the whole truth. One clear sign of this is the opening passage of section A, which appears to introduce the Four Gentlemen by name as they arrive at the court of the Liang emperor Wu, but in fact leaves out much of the detail. Far more detail emerges in quotations found in three other Song sources, all notebook-style works dealing with literary and historical topics.[10] If the opening of the book available to those authors was pruned down in *Extensive records*, or even in its source, how much else might have been pruned down as well? One most obvious gap is the end of the work. As you will see, we don't really know how the book concluded: it was clearly both episodic and structured, but the question of an ending, so crucial to the way we read it, is left open.

Here is how the notebook texts introduce the Four Gentlemen of Liang:[11]

> In the Datong period[12] the emperor [Wu] humbly and respectfully entertained scholars. There suddenly appeared four men who looked some seventy years of age, shuffling along dressed in rags. They entered Jiankang village in Danyang commandery,[13] where for years they lived by begging without being recognized.
>
> While the emperor dwelt in the Tongtai monastery to discourse upon Buddhist scriptures, Sengcuo and Sengzao of Yongan understood his subtle arguments to perfection and engaged in debate with him. But when the four men together came to pay respects, the two monks held their tongue.[14]
>
> The emperor was startled and summoned them into the Yixian hall, provided them with hot water for washing, and removed some of the imperial garments to bestow on them.[15] When he asked them about the Three Doctrines, the Nine Schools and the past affairs of the Han dynasty, it was just as if those things were right there in front of him. The emperor found this extraordinary and asked their names. One was named Xi Chen, of a Sunyang family; one named Wan Jie, of a Tianqi family; one named Shu Tuan, of a Gaomen family; one named Zhang Du, of a Wuruan family.[16]
>
> No one in court knew them but the Crown Prince Zhaoming, who recognized and treated them with ceremony and respect.[17] The four men delightedly bowed to him as an old acquaintance, and they became known at the time as the Four Noblemen.

From this point on we depend entirely on the *Extensive records*.

Let me explain here that the Four Gentlemen now introduced to us belong to that trying sort of people who know your business better than you do yourself. Worse than that, they show no inclination to conceal the fact. Worst of all, they always turn out to be right. And that is not my sardonic observation on the narrative content of *The Four Gentlemen of Liang*, it is a perception expressly brought out in the text of the book itself. This consists of a rich series of episodes in which anyone at court with a claim to authority on some subject (not excluding the emperor himself) is ruthlessly, or even fatally, humiliated by the superior knowledge of one of the Four Gentlemen. The story makes them come out to bat in turn, and each of them specializes in one general area of knowledge. Xi Chen knows about divination; Shu Tuan knows about historical precedent; Wan Jie knows about foreign regions and natural products; Zhang Du knows how to conduct learned debate. So the text naturally delivers a great display of exotic knowledge and uncanny skill, but it also expresses the pain and resentment felt by emperor, courtiers, ambassadors and commoners forced to witness and suffer that display. My eventual question will be: Why? What point is being made here? And I shall suggest that the book presents even more ambiguity on this matter than first appears.

I have described the book as structured as well as episodic. There are four gentlemen, and they each perform, according to section A, in turn. Four is unlikely to be a random number. There is an echo, perhaps implicit, perhaps explicit in a lost part of the text, of the Warring States 'Four Noble Sons, known as Chunshen, Pingyuan, Mengchang, and Xinling',[18] whose fame in Chinese tradition had to do with their patronage of talented knights. Another point arises from the gentlemen's places of origin, which appear only in one of the notebook sources:[19] they are obscure places, requiring specialized glosses, but they do suggest a matching with the directions north, south, east and west. All that gives a sense of schematic structure. But quite possibly the text implies a more narrative-determined structure, too. To explain that I must describe the first episode.

In section A it begins without further ado when the emperor commands the courtier Shen Yue[20] to prepare an object for use in a guessing game with his officials. The game is called *she fu*. It involves covering over an object, then holding a competition to disclose by divination what the object is. So the name *she fu* means something like 'targeting under cover'. In the dynastic histories this court game is documented from the second century BC down to the third century AD. The imperial library of the Liang dynasty held books containing the same expression in their titles. For the Tang there is a record that when forty two specialist practitioners in the Hanlin Academy were dismissed in 786, they included *she fu* experts along with physiognomists and stargazers.[21] But this passage from *The Four Gentlemen of Liang* may be the only place in Chinese literature to give a very detailed description of what went on.

This is what happens. Someone has caught a rat. Shen Yue ties it up inside a box and submits the box to the throne. The emperor performs a milfoil divination, deduces a hexagram and privately formulates his interpretation. Then eight ministers are commanded to perform divinations and leave the results with the emperor. And now one of the Four Gentlemen, Master Xi Chen, is told to draw the milfoil stalks. But he insists on using the emperor's own divination as the basis for his interpretation. He too leaves the result on the emperor's private mat with the rest and withdraws. We are then treated to the full text of the emperor's interpretation, which uses symbolism based upon the hexagrams of the *Book of changes* to deduce that the object must be a dead rat.

'The whole body of officials,' we read, 'danced in salutation as they applauded the emperor. The emperor in their midst commended his own abilities, wearing a very pleased expression.' Next they read out the texts of eight ministers' interpretations. Some have analysed in terms of colour, some have drawn inferences about energy, some have taken a meaning from the signs, some from the hexagram lines, some have used imagery of birds and beasts, turtles and dragons, *yin* and *yang* flying up or lying hidden. But none has got the right answer. Now it is time to read out Master Xi Chen's interpretation. This is given in full technical detail, and eventually draws the conclusion that the hidden object is four live rats, which will however die when the sun goes down. Let me quote the passage which now follows:

> Once they beheld a live rat the officials went pale and berated Master Chen in these terms: "Your interpretation included four rats, but now there is only one. Why is that?" Master [Chen] said: "Can it please be dissected?" But the emperor was by nature averse to killing, and felt resentment that he had failed to guess correctly himself. When the time came for the sun to set the rat did indeed die. So the order was given to dissect it, and sure enough it was pregnant with three young.[22]

The narrative is carefully constructed so that we, the readers, know part of the answer in advance, but not the whole answer. And the partial answer corresponds quite closely to emperor Wu's interpretation. His officials behave impeccably by producing stylish but incorrect answers, leaving the emperor to bask in his superiority. But Xi Chen subverts the whole courtly equilibrium by outsmarting the emperor, the courtiers, and ourselves the readers.

The consequences are interesting. Instead of going on to another such episode, the narrative tells us:

> On that day the emperor moved the Four Gentlemen over to the west tower of the Wuming Hall: outwardly a sign of more intimate proximity, but in reality keeping them confined. Only at new moon and full moon, on the *fu* days and the *la* days were they allowed to meet the whole body of scholars in the Yixian chamber. However, they were always consulted by any who had doubtful points in military or national affairs.

Specialist knowledge of divination was politically threatening in imperial China, and indeed the historical emperor Wu of Liang was one of those who took steps to remove books of divination from public circulation.[23] So the Four Gentlemen are treated as potentially dangerous characters, much as our governments might regard rocket scientists or nuclear fission experts.

This, I suggest, looks like the first leg of a narrative structure. It leads us to expect some later developments. It seems unlikely that the Four Gentlemen will simply go on upsetting people with their superior knowledge until the author tires of writing about them. We want to know how their career in court will end, whether they will play a role in the terrible events that will later overtake the Liang dynasty – the devastating rebellion of Hou Jing, the humiliating death of the aged emperor Wu in his rebel-occupied palace, the disgrace of the emperor Yuan's collapse before the Western Wei at Jiangling, and the sweeping away of the Liang dynasty in the south. Section B of the surviving text does mention the Hou Jing rebellion,[24] but no other hint of those events remains.

If structure there was, it raises more immediate questions concerning the three sections A, B and C, and how they might have fitted together in the source text that came down to the tenth century. A is by far the most substantial, and might almost stand alone as a narrative of the Four Gentlemen of Liang. It is 3,000 characters long, and appears in the chapters of *Extensive records* devoted to extraordinary men (*yi ren*). Within one span of narrative it presents the first appearance of the group of four, then, in order, the divination exploit of Master Xi Chen, a protocol dispute with Master Shu Tuan concerning the reception of foreign ambassadors, a series of confrontations between Master Wan Jie and visiting ambassadors concerning the tribute offerings they have brought, and finally a grand set-piece debate on every branch of learning between Master Zhang Du and Cui Min, a diplomatic visitor from the Eastern Wei. It is Master Zhang Du's comprehensive victory in this duel of words, literally a fight to the death, that brings the narrative of section A to a close. It ends with the words: 'Now that Cui Min's eloquence had been broken by Du he had lost his self-respect. Consequently he fell ill and took to his carriage. But before completing his journey back north, he died on the road.' Were those really the closing words of *The Four Gentlemen of Liang*? Does section A give the true shape of that lost book?

There is of course the matter of sections B and C. They both appear side by side in a completely different part of the *Extensive records*, the first of its chapters on dragons. Section B is relatively short, 227 characters in length, and gives an account of a remarkable coloured stone presented to the throne by a hermit: Master Wan Jie recognizes it as 'a stone of the life-transforming dragons in the upper world', and he gives expert advice on how to prepare it for carving into bowls. Eventually one of the dragons comes down to remove the remaining pieces of stone. The bowls, we are told, vanish in the course of the Hou Jing rebellion.

Now follows section C, some 1100 characters long. It tells a more involved tale about a quest to obtain rare pearls from an underwater store in the charge of the Eastern Ocean dragon king's seventh daughter. This again falls within Master Wan Jie's sphere of knowledge. He knows exactly how to prepare for the expedition, what equipment to take, what gifts and bribes will find a way past the thousands of dragons which guard the pearls. And when these are successfully brought back, it is Master Wan Jie who knows how to appraise and test them. The narrative is deliberately and remarkably rich in cultural detail, and will repay study from many points of view.[25] But its display of exotic technical knowledge in a drama of confrontation in court, followed by empirical verification, is the essential texture of *The Four Gentlemen of Liang*.

If section A gives, apart from a substantial body of text, also a framework for the work as a whole, then how do sections B and C fit into it? They both feature Master Wan Jie: so if the source-work was structured to give each of the Four Gentlemen a self-standing group of episodes, these two must also belong with the 'Wan Jie' group in section A. They differ from that group by dealing with topics other than ambassadorial tribute, but the focus of interest is basically the same. Adding them to this part of section A does create a heavily unbalanced narrative: Master Wan Jie already occupies more than half the text in section A; with sections B and C as well, his group of episodes dominates the work. But he would dominate it wherever we chose to place those two sections.

It is difficult to see an alternative structure. Section A presents its events consistently with chronology recorded elsewhere.[26] It is impossible to justify any internal reorganization. To create a balance there instead by imagining lengthy batches of lost episodes associated with the other three gentlemen would be pushing hypothesis into the realm of guesswork.

What we have is coherent text amounting to 4300 characters,

a not inadequate amount for a one-scroll work. But what we lack is anything that could guide us in placing this remarkable fragment in a meaningful literary and historical context. The evidence on authorship has been confused for the past thousand years, and it offers little more than bare names. Chen Zhensun enticingly refers to a passage at the end of the copy he owned which described transmission of the material to Liang Zaiyan by Tian Tong of Zichuan. But Tian Tong is unknown to history, and Liang Zaiyan is quite obscure. Chen Zhensun's private catalogue records his metropolitan graduation in 675; the two *Histories of the Tang* sketch an official career in the courts of Empress Wu and the emperor Zhong zong, ending as prefect of Huai zhou; there are bibliographical entries for three books by him, which seem to have been compendia of official personnel records and administrative geography.[27] If this is the man associated with *The Four Gentlemen of Liang*, he was a contemporary of Zhang Yue, the other name associated with that book, in the late seventh and early eighth centuries. But no early preface or colophon survives to guide us further.

The medieval catalogues and bibliographies shed very little light on what kind of book this was. One early reference to the title, in a preface to a collection of tales written towards the end of the eighth century, puts it in a loosely assembled list of works by 'men who recorded the anomalous'.[28] But the *New history of the Tang* in 1060 classifies it in the Histories division under 'miscellaneous transmitted records', then Chen Zhensun in the mid-thirteenth century as 'transmitted records', echoed again in the fourteenth century by two derivative works – the great documentary compendium *General examination of standard writings* and the *History of the Song*.[29] In all these cases the book keeps company with a most heterogeneous collection of titles, in which the common ground is nothing more precise than their unofficial status.

There was in medieval bibliography a fundamental uncertainty in classifying informal narrative literature. The entrenched classing of all writings in four divisions created difficult choices in practice for bibliographers looking at what was really a very diverse and irregular mass of items. Should a given item be assigned to Histories, within which subdivisions would then have to be created to handle the oddities? Or should it go under Masters, which traditionally accommodated all kinds of specialist or technical writing – a home, then, for eccentric books? Zheng Qiao, author of the *General record*, explained the problem in his own words:

> In bibliography, from ancient times until now, there are five categories which cannot be separated – the first is 'Transmitted records' (*zhuan ji*), the second 'Miscellaneous schools' (*za jia*), the third 'Commonplaces' (*xiaoshuo*), the fourth 'Miscellaneous histories' (*za shi*), the fifth 'Ancient matters' (*gu shi*). All books in those five categories are likely to be confused together.[30]

He frankly admits that here classification cannot control the complexities of actual written production. But what for the bibliographer may seem a matter for despair can also be seen as the sign of a rich, varied and intricately articulated literature.

The Four Gentlemen of Liang must have appeared too late in the eighth century to attract the attention of Liu Zhiji (661-721), whose *Anatomy of histories* was completed in 710. Liu's fastidious and ruthless discrimination in assessing individual works by the criteria he set for the historian's profession would surely have drawn from him some pungent and illuminating comment on this one.[31] The loss to us is severe, since we can't turn to any critic of comparable calibre for a view on how a work like this could stand classification as a history. Even Chen Zhensun, who spurned the contents as too wild and extravagant to be worth scrutiny, acquiesced in the same classification. As with the other titles in that class, this was a gesture of indifference or of despair.

For Chinese scholarship in the 1990s the problem seems no longer to exist. The literary historian Hou Zhongyi has no hesitation in classifying this book as 'a typical work from the evolutionary period of the *chuanqi*', and for him the *chuanqi* is that innovation of Tang narrative art which involved both fictional creation and coherent structure.[32] He sums up like this:

> As an early work in the development of *chuanqi*, *The Four Gentlemen of Liang*, though already possessing the form of a

chuanqi, still lacks close interconnection of its narrative content. Under one main heading it is actually formed of a large number of independent little stories. But despite its limited artistic achievement, *The Four Gentlemen of Liang*, like many other works of the same period, built up experience and laid foundations for the arrival of the high point in the development of the *chuanqi*.[33]

This entirely formal analysis accepts the tyranny of one generic term with which to measure the narrative achievements of the Tang period, and it was not even a term which Tang writers themselves used in a generic sense. While the medieval bibliographers wrestled with interesting complexity, the 1990s sweep everything into one or two simple categories.

Another modern historian of medieval narrative literature, Li Jianguo, is also content to give this book the simple formal label '*chuanqi* text'.[34] But he is more absorbed by the question of authorship, and uses the catalogue evidence to construct an intuitive judgement. He fully endorses the ascription of this book to Zhang Yue, points out that it does contain certain historically verifiable details alongside the 'wild and extravagant' material, but finds some further implied significance there. He reflects on certain phrases in the *Old history of the Tang* biography of Zhang Yue, which represent that famous statesman as 'leading men of letters to lend support to kingly culture: with peace established for long years, his aim lay in adorning the glorious age'.[35] Li concludes:

> This memoir narrates how, in the age of emperor Wu of Liang, remarkable men assembled and valuable objects came in. An ancient precedent is used to praise the magnificence of the Tang court. That surely is what it means?[36]

This deeply learned scholar has allowed a circumstantial link with the stately Zhang Yue to tempt him into interpreting simply by authorial intention. But looking again at the fragments of *The Four Gentlemen of Liang*, I find them astonishingly discordant with his reading. The text itself unsettles any attempt to place it neatly within this or any other familiar category of writing. It creates its own mystery.

If there is one discordant quality which runs through every part of the fragmentary text, it is irony. Irony is here at all levels: it undermines and subverts any straightforward interpretation. First the irony of history, which itself works at more than one level. It was impossible for a Tang writer to tell of the splendours of the Liang emperor Wu's reign without being aware that it ended in violence, massive destruction, humiliation and death. We have seen that the bowls made from the emperor's dragon-stone vanished during the Hou Jing rebellion: this author knew exactly what was coming. So just what was the comparison with emperor Wu intended to convey with reference to the Tang court? Was it really such a complimentary comparison? This is one level of historical irony. But there is another. With the hindsight of the Song, and much more with our own long-term hindsight, the comparison of the Tang emperor Xuan zong's court to that of emperor Wu of the Liang *was* bitterly appropriate: both regimes high points in the history of Chinese culture, both emperors great cultural icons in the sight of later ages, and both destroyed by political rebellion and civil war, leaving fragile and ultimately doomed polities behind them. What celebration is this?

Even without the circumstantial historical ironies, more immediate ones bristle everywhere in the text. The historical emperor Wu was not only a ruler who presided for long years over a kingdom of brilliant cultural achievements, and who later had legendary status in the history of Chinese Buddhist ritual, he was a figure of intellectual authority in medieval China. That, however, is not how he appears in *The Four Gentlemen of Liang*. He appears there virtually as a comic opera character, helplessly vulnerable to contemptuous manipulation by the Four Gentlemen. Here is an episode in which he is in direct confrontation with Master Shu Tuan over the reception of foreign embassies:

> The emperor asked the Four Gentlemen: "[Representatives of] foreign lands have come to court. In what concerns insignia of rank, high or low, I wish to accord them the precedence of senior dukes."

Master Tuan said: "... If you rank [these ambassadors] as senior dukes, I fear that cannot be documented in antiquity."

The emperor was firmly convinced that Master Tuan had settled the matter even more thoroughly. But presently there came a powerful wind, spinning like a wheel, which tugged at the emperor's skirt and sash. The emperor inquired about this event too.

Master [Tuan] said: "Things will not come to pass tomorrow. Please let the discussions take place on some other day."

The emperor was displeased, and all the scholars reviled [Master Tuan]. But towards evening the emperor's daughter fell from a tower and died. So the [ambassadorial] rites were not carried out.

When questioned later, [Master Tuan] said: "When a whirlwind attacks your clothing, your beloved child will meet a violent end. What further doubt could there be?"[37]

Is this the celebration of a splendid age? Would the Tang emperors have been flattered by comparisons like this?

If we turn to the valuable objects pouring into the Liang court during emperor Wu's reign, the same dark shadows come out of the narrative. Here is a passage about the embassy from Turfan:

> The land of Turfan sent ambassadors to offer in tribute:– two lumps of salt, each the size of a wine vat, in appearance as white as jade; raisins; thorn honey; frozen wine; white-wheat flour. Monarch, courtiers and people all failed to recognize these things ... The emperor ordered Master [Wan] Jie to receive them. [Wan Jie] said to the ambassadors: "One piece of salt was collected at the full moon on the Southern Burnt Sheep Mountain, one on the Northern Burnt Sheep Mountain, but not at the full moon. Of the raisins, seven [tenths] are Wulin and three [tenths] are Wuban. The frozen wine was not frozen in the Valley of the Eight Winds, and furthermore has been mixed with Gaoning wine. The thorn honey was produced in Yancheng [county], not in Nanping town. The white wheat flour is from Dangchang, not the genuine article from Changlei."
>
> The ambassadors gave a full account of the true facts. The flour's colour had been spoiled by the passage of a year, so they had filled in [some more] by trading when they reached

Dangchang. There had been disastrous winds that year, and the grapes and thorn honey had not ripened – hence the adulterations. As for the salt and the frozen wine, they were out of season because the king's urgent command had to be obeyed.

Then he asked about purple salt and medicinal amber.

They said that those had been seized in the middle of their journey by the Northern Liang[38] – they had not ventured to speak of this.[39]

Master Wan Jie goes on at length about the tribute articles, what they should be like, and how these fall short of acceptable standards. It is, as usual, a prodigious display of knowledge, but hardly a celebration of tributary splendours.

The debate scene which concludes section A is more openly menacing.[40] The background is an era in the 530s when the courts of the Eastern Wei and the Liang celebrate scholars for their abilities in quick response. Master Zhang Du is a front-line performer, who, it says, 'made the other side captive to his arts and constantly broke their verbal barbs, with no device deployed in vain.' But in 541 two men come on a diplomatic visit from the Eastern Wei – Cui Min and Yang Xiuzhi. Cui Min's scholarly skills are outstanding, and include the arts of astronomy, musical and calendrical science, healing and medication, and divination. He humbles the eighteen Buddhist monks selected by emperor Wu to debate with him. But the Four Gentlemen come forward to propose: "If you command your servant [Zhang] Du to take him on, he will surely die." That, in brief, is what happens: humiliation in debate does lead to Cui Min's death on the road home to Wei.

The episode as a whole sets up an intriguing parallel with recorded history: there really was a Cui Min of the Eastern Wei; he really was sent with Yang Xiuzhi on a diplomatic visit to Liang in that year; he did possess the scholarly skills listed out in *The Four Gentlemen of Liang*; and he did die, aged 27, on the way home in 541.[41] But the dynastic histories make no mention of debating: instead they disclose that Cui Min foresaw his own demise before leaving for Liang.[42] The debate and its causal relationship with Cui Min's death remain open questions. But this part of the narrative differs from the others in *The Four Gentlemen of Liang*: it represents the debate by telling, rather than showing, the reader. There is a list of the vast range of topics covered, but no direct taste of the debate itself. Instead it is the prediction of death and its fulfilment that give shape to the whole scene.

If anything is being celebrated here it is a triumph of superior knowledge and forensic skill. And it is comprehensive secular knowledge, not divinely inspired religious power, that wins the day. The text almost asks to be read as an affirmation of science as a higher value than temporal power or ritual decorum. Yet there too a possible irony gets in the way. My last quotation comes from a scene in court during which Master Wan Jie has made a long speech outlining the wonders of lands in the four quarters of the earth. There is (for instance) a sea of milk, enclosing fertile lands where "great ducks give birth to fine horses and great birds give birth to humans; the boys die, but the girls live, and the birds carry away their daughters in their beaks, feeding them as they fly; if they cannot manage the load in their beaks they carry them on their backs." And so on.

> When the court heard this speech they clapped their hands and guffawed in derision, regarding it as so much mystification and fantasy. They said: "This is no more than the talk you find in Zou Yan's Nine Continents and Wang Jia's *Records of neglected things gathered up*."[43]

The courtier Wang Yun[44] then challenges Master Wan Jie on the basis of received knowledge in written tradition, contradicting points of information.[45] He coolly responds with even fuller detail on the disputed points. Then, gradually, events unfold (arrival of embassies, and suchlike) which one by one prove Master Wan Jie's words empirically correct. And his section of the text ends with the comment: 'Only now did the dignitaries of the Liang court believe that Master [Wan] Jie had travelled to all quarters of the earth, was at home in all ages of the past, and that his words were not empty talk, but all fine discourse.'[46]

The whole episode deserves thinking through quite carefully.

This is a narrative which acknowledges a full-blown sceptical position, which allows the cosmographic teachings of Zou Yan in the third century BC and the data-collection of Wang Jia in the fourth century AD to be scorned as 'mystification'. It represents the Liang court, the most catholic and sophisticated intellectual milieu of pre-Tang China, as setting aside an earlier literature characterized as 'fantasy' to take a more critical position. But it then goes on to represent that same court allowing itself to be convinced by a series of events and reports unfolding in its midst. What rational men earlier dismissed as fantasy is now imposed by the narrative as secure fact.

Dizzying ironies are at work here. If we take *The Four Gentlemen of Liang* as frankly a work of exuberant fantasy, then what we have just read can only be an ironical and playful teasing of the reader, in effect deconstructing the whole text. If we take it that the book delivers statements held true by the author as a matter of solemn conviction, we have only to wait for the Song to see the whole thing waved aside. Is it even possible for us, as modern readers, to know what thoughts this book communicated to its early readers on the subject of duck/horses and such matters? Did they quickly and easily see a disjunction between believable reality and a dazzling construct of fantasy? Was this then a work of amusing escapism, a kind of medieval science fiction? Or was the whole business more serious for them? Or again, was there a mixed audience, divided between those who read one way and those who read another? Was there, finally, a project of satire here, the point of which remains concealed from us?

I offer no answers to these questions. My point here is that we have discovered the sense in which this book is truly lost. The fragments that do remain simply fail to associate it clearly with any known or acknowledged genre of medieval literature. It does have roots in a range of earlier works, some of which it signals openly itself – the cosmographic writings of Zou Yan (vividly described in the *Records of the Grand Historian*,[47] but now quite lost), and the literature of anomaly which developed through the post-Han period – but also in the established culture of court debate and polemic. Yet those external and internal ironies set it apart from them all, as they do from the '*chuanqi*' label so favoured by modern critics.

Such uncertainties make clear just how rudderless modern readers are without those adjuncts which point and guide the text of more fully transmitted narrative works from the Tang – above all the moralistic postscripts in which authors adopt the mode of judgement and speak with the voice of transmitters, but also the prefaces in which contemporaries reflect on and respond to the themes of given works. In their absence historical reading becomes problematic. Catalogues and classifications from later times, even when based on first-hand contact with the books, just do not fill the gap.

☆

It is the fate of transmitted books to be traduced as they are transmitted. Something like that happened to *The Four Gentlemen of Liang*. By the thirteenth century this book engaged the curiosity of Chen Zhensun with the puzzle of its authorship, but its contents were too wild and extravagant to be worth his scrutiny. It survived the Song period only through the fragments described here today – in other words through a tenth-century source which had cut the book into pieces and distributed them, quite likely in condensed form, to different parts of an encyclopedic classification. Section A survived there because it illustrated a group of 'Extraordinary men', sections B and C because they had thematic links with dragons. The book had here already lost its unity and now embarked on a further process of decay. We can watch that set in one more stage with the fate of section C in the mid-sixteenth century, when it reappeared, textually even more condensed, as a tale of the dragon maiden of Zhenze Lake in a collection called *The ocean of tales ancient and modern*.[48] The textual debt to *The Four Gentlemen of Liang* is not even acknowledged there, and the missing context of the story leaves its main feature, the brilliance of Master Wan Jie, quite unintelligible.[49]

A book transmitted in such a way can't be said to survive. A better way to describe it, in the language of the late twentieth century, would be 'recycled'. In the sight of what Donald McKenzie called 'degressive bibliography'[50] the book's remains are distorted, misshapen stumps of a ruined structure. Or, to use a milder image, they give partial glimpses in soft focus of a work that was once there. But in the eyes of the more open, inclusive bibliographical thinking launched by McKenzie and others, these remnants represent the last flickering attempts of late-medieval and early modern compilers and anthologists to discover some significance in a subversive, unsettling text from the past.

Subject classification did not ensure the survival of *Summary documents of three kingdoms*, nor has it illuminated the remains of *The Four Gentlemen of Liang*. But those two books do between them demonstrate the potentials and the limitations of Chinese textual tradition in recovering loss over the past thousand years. Thanks to Song Tai zong's library and his compilers, medieval literature can still show a richer and a more challenging aspect than transmitted books would otherwise suggest.

NOTES

1 *Tong zhi* 71.2a. The passage is quoted from that work's monograph on critical bibliography, 'Jiao chou lüe 校讎略', and discussed above in Lecture I, p. 12. See also discussion in Glen Dudbridge, 'A question of classification in Tang narrative: the story of Ding Yue' in Alfredo Cadonna, ed., *India, Tibet, China: genesis and aspects of traditional narrative*, Florence 1999, pp. 152–3.

2 The specific terminology used in the title of the work, including the terms translated here as 'documents' (*dian* 典) and 'summary' (*lüe* 略), and its classification in catalogues of the Song period, are discussed in Du Deqiao and Zhao Chao, *Sanguo dian lüe*, '*Sanguo dian lüe* gailun', pp. 6 ff.

3 Li Jianguo 李劍國 in *Tang Wudai zhiguai chuanqi xulu* 唐五代志怪傳奇敍錄, vol. 1, Tianjin 1993, p. 148, cites literary references which suggest that the work was still seen during the Yuan period (1278-1368).

4 *Zhizhai shulu jieti* 直齋書錄解題 7.196: ed. Xu Xiaoman 徐小蠻 and Gu Meihua 顧美華, Shanghai 1987.

5 The date of Zhang Yue's 張說 death, according to his tomb inscription by Zhang Jiuling 張九齡 in *Wen yuan ying hua* 文苑英華, repr. Beijing 1966, 936.4a, was Kaiyuan 18/12/*wushen* 午申 [9 February 731]. See Paul W. Kroll, 'On the date of Chang Yüeh's death', *Chinese Literature: Essays, Articles and Reviews* 2, 1980, 264–5.

6 The *Zhongxing guange shumu* 中興館閣書目, now mostly lost. See note 8 to Lecture II.

7 *Xin Tang shu* 58.1484. For Liang Zaiyan's 梁載言 brief biographies see *Jiu Tang shu* 190B.5017 and *Xin Tang shu* 202.5753. He

received the *jinshi* 進士 degree in 675, and ended his official career under Zhong zong 中宗 (705–710) as prefect of Huai zhou 懷州.

8 The *Handan tushu zhi* 邯鄲圖書志 by Li Shu 李淑, now lost. See Piet van der Loon, *Taoist books in the libraries of the Sung period*, p. 24.

9 *Taiping guang ji* 81.517–522 (A); 418.3403–4 (B); 418.3404–6 (C).

10 *Liuchao shiji bian lei* 六朝事跡編類 by Zhang Dunyi 張敦頤 (degree in 1138): ed. Zhang Chenshi 張忱石, Shanghai 1995, 4.53; *Yunlu man chao* 雲麓漫鈔 by Zhao Yanwei 趙彥衛: Shanghai 1957, 6.91–92; *Wenchang za lu* 文昌雜錄 by Pang Yuanying 龐元英: Shanghai 1958, 6.73.

11 The narrative as translated here is assembled by blending material from *Liuchao shiji bian lei* and *Yunlu man chao*. *Wenchang za lu* contributes only the material described in note 17, below.

12 Datong 大通, corresponding to 527–529. *Taiping guang ji* 81.517 gives Tianjian 天監 (502–519).

13 During the Southern Dynasties this was an administration in the vicinity of the city Jianye 建業, later Jiankang 建康. By late Tang times the site of the administrative centre was within Shangyuan 上元 county, Runzhou 潤州 prefecture: *Yuanhe jun xian tu zhi* 元和郡縣圖志, by Li Jifu 李吉甫 (758–814), ed. He Cijun 賀次君, Beijing 1983, 25.594.

14 For *zhu kou* 柱口 I read *zhu kou* 住口. The text in this paragraph appears only in *Yunlu man chao*.

15 *Jie yu fu ci zhi* 解御服賜之: phrase supplied from *Liuchao shiji bian lei*.

16 Phonetic glosses to the personal names (not always the same) are given in *Yunlu man chao*, *Wenchang za lu*, and *Taiping guang ji*

81.517. The lineage choronyms are given only in *Wenchang za lu*: see next note.

17 *Wenchang za lu* includes a passage in which the Crown Prince gives canonical or literary antecedents for each unusual character in their names and glosses the lineage choronyms. He identifies Sunyuan 孫原 as a mountain in the Bo 僰 country (deep south-west), Gaomen as the names of two rivers between the Tao 洮 and the Huang 湟 (both tributaries of the Yellow River in its upper reaches in Central Asia), and Wuruan 五阮 as Yanmen 雁門, the mountain range on the traditional northern border of the Han peoples in Shanxi. Tianqi 天齊 was a name given to Tai shan 泰山 and to a stream running south of Linzi 臨淄 in Shandong. The Crown Prince Zhaoming 昭明太子 is best known to posterity as Xiao Tong 蕭統, the compiler of the standard literary anthology *Wen xuan* 文選. His appearance in this narrative has implications for its internal dating. He died in 531 at the age of 31 *sui*, and was therefore born in 501 (*Liang shu* 8.169). The dating to Datong given in *Liuchao shiji bian lei* and *Yunlu man chao* would allow him the relatively mature age of 27 or 28 when the Four Gentlemen first appeared in court. But the narrative later also allows for the participation of Shen Yue 沈約, who died in 513, when the Crown Prince would still be a child of 12 or 13: this would be more consistent with the Tianjian dating given in *Taiping guang ji* (see note 12, above, and note 20, below).

18 For this see *Yunlu man chao* 6.91, where the Warring States group is used as a way of introducing the Four Gentlemen of Liang. It seems most plausible to read these opening words as an introduction by the Song author Zhao Yanwei, but they could conceivably have appeared in *Liang si gong ji*.

19 *Wenchang za lu* 6.73.
20 The appearance in the text of Shen Yue (441–513), an important literary figure associated with the origins of tonal euphony in Chinese prosody and author of the standard dynastic history *Song shu* 宋書, has implications here for internal dating. Shen Yue served at the court of three southern dynasties – Song, Qi and Liang – but died during the Tianjian period of emperor Wu's reign (502–519). This is consistent with the dating given in *Taiping guang ji*, but not with that given in *Yunlu man chao* and *Liuchao shiji bianlei*: see notes 12 and 17, above.
21 See references in note 25 to Lecture I.
22 For this episode, see *Taiping guang ji* 81.517–8.
23 *Sui shu* 32.941. The passage records the Sui emperor Yang's purge of apocryphal prophetic texts, but actually traces imperial suppression of these texts back to the Southern Dynasties: the Daming 大明 period of Song (457–464) and Tianjian period of the Liang (502–519).
24 *Taiping guang ji* 418.3403–4.
25 An example is the man who volunteers to go and seek the pearls from the dragons (*Taiping guang ji* 418.3404–5). Luo Zichun 羅子春 and his brothers are natives of Leizhou peninsula, the land of the pearl fisheries in medieval China (E. H. Schafer, 'The pearl fisheries of Ho-p'u', *Journal of the American Oriental Society* 72, 1952, 155–168), and they claim kinship with territorial dragons of Hainan Island and the Luofu Mountains east of Guangzhou. They belong to that population of southern tribal peoples over whom the Chinese state was barely imposing its control in the early Tang, let alone the Liang two centuries before. Already in *Shi ji*, Beijing 1959, 43.1808, the ethnic name Ouyue 甌越 had referred to the tattooed and crop-haired

people of the far south; the lost text *Yu di zhi* 輿地志 cited in *Shi ji zhengyi* 史記正義, ib. 43.1809, recorded their antagonism to dragons; they were associated with Zhuyai 珠崖 commandery, now Hainan Island: see *Shi ji suoyin* 史記索隱, ib. In pre-Tang and Tang texts they appeared in literary tropes invoking the geographical extremes of the south and east: see *Jin shu* 晉書 28.848; *Liang shu* 56.839; *Wei shu* 97.2144; *Bei Qi shu* 3.35. To see characters like this with their mythological pedigree as it was perceived by a writer in the eighth century is of genuine historical interest.

26 Taken at face value, the contents of the text allow for both a date before the death of Shen Yue in 513 (cf. note 20) and a date after the death of Cui Min in 541 (see note 41). The embassies from the lands of Panpan 盤盤, Dandan 丹丹 and Gaochang 高昌, which form the subject of the emperor's exchange with Master Shu Tuan, are dated in the text to the Datong 大同 period [535–546]; the dynastic histories record embassies from Panpan in 527, 529, 532 and 534, from Dandan in 531 (variant 530) and 535, and from Gaochang in the Datong 大同 period: see *Nan shi* 78.1958, 1959, and 79.1984; *Liang shu* 54.793, 794. Master Zhang Du's debate with Cui Min of the Eastern Wei is dated in the text to 540/541. Section B does of course refer retrospectively to the Hou Jing rebellion, reaching the capital in 548.

27 *Jiu Tang shu* 190B.5017; *Xin Tang shu* 202.5753, also 58.1477, 1484, 1506; *Zhizhai shulu jieti* 6.173 and 239. Remains of his administrative geography, *Shi dao zhi* 十道志, were collected by Wang Mo 王謨 in *Han Tang dili shu chao* 漢唐地理書鈔, repr. Beijing 1961, pp. 267-90; and by Wang Renjun 王仁俊 in *Yu han shanfang jiyi shu bubian* 玉函山房輯佚書補編.

28 Preface to Dai Fu's 戴孚 *Guang yi ji* 廣異記 by Gu Kuang 顧況, in *Wen yuan ying hua* 文苑英華 737.6b. For a translation and analysis of this document see Glen Dudbridge, *Religious experience and lay society in T'ang China: a reading of Tai Fu's Kuang-i chi*, Cambridge 1995, pp. 18–45. Gu Kuang associates *Liang si gong zhuan* 梁四公傳 with an author named [Duke of] Yan 燕 (the character *gong* 公, 'duke', is absent in *Wen yuan ying hua* 737.6b, but supplied in *Quan Tang wen* 全唐文, imperial edn. repr. Taibei 1965, 528.14b). This title was borne by Zhang Yue from 713: *Jiu Tang shu* 8.171, 97.3052; *Wen yuan ying hua* 936.4a.

29 *Xin Tang shu* 58.1484: *za zhuan ji* 雜傳記; *Zhizhai shulu jieti* 7.196; *Wenxian tong kao* 198.5b–6a; *Song shi* 203.5111. On the sources of the latter, compare note 26 to Lecture I.

30 *Tong zhi* 71.17a.

31 On Liu Zhiji 劉知幾 and the *Shi tong* 史通, see Michael Quirin, *Liu Zhiji und das Chun Qiu*, Würzburger Sino-Japonica 15, Frankfurt am Main, etc., 1987; also E. G. Pulleyblank, 'Chinese historical criticism: Liu Chih-chi and Ssu-ma Kuang', pp. 136 ff. Liu Zhiji certainly turned his attention to many other titles listed in the preface by Gu Kuang: see above, note 28.

32 Hou Zhongyi 侯忠義, *Sui Tang Wudai xiaoshuo shi* 随唐五代小說史, Hangzhou 1997, pp. 1–2, 36.

33 *Ibid.*, p. 38.

34 Li Jianguo, *Tang wudai zhiguai chuanqi xulu*, vol. I, p. 145.

35 *Jiu Tang shu* 97.3057.

36 Li Jianguo, p. 150.

37 *Taiping guang ji* 81.518–9.

38 The brief Northern Liang 北涼 kingdom of the Xiongnu 匈奴 people, situated along the Gansu corridor, lasted only from 397 to

439, when it was annexed by the Northern Wei. It had thus been extinct for a hundred years before the recorded embassy from Turfan [Gaochang] in the time of emperor Wu of the Liang: cf. above, note 26.

39 *Taiping guang ji* 81.519.
40 *Taiping guang ji* 81.522.
41 Biographies of Cui Min 崔㥄 (514–541), more usually referred to by his style Changqian 長謙: *Wei shu* 69.1528, *Bei shi* 24.879–80; embassy to Liang on Xinghe 興和 2/12/12 [24 January 541]: *Wei shu* 12.304, 69.1528, *Liang shu* 39.555, *Bei Qi shu* 42.562, *Bei shi* 5.189, 19.693, 24.880; accompanied by Yang Xiuzhi 陽休之: *Bei Qi shu* 42.562; scholarly attainments: *Bei shi* 24.879–80; death on road: *Wei shu* 69.1528, *Bei shi* 24.880. Yang Xiuzhi (509–582) was an influential figure who held office under the Northern Wei, Eastern Wei, Northern Qi, Zhou and Sui dynasties: *Bei Qi shu* 42.560–64; *Bei shi* 47.1724–8.
42 *Bei shi* 24.880: 'On the point of departure he said to someone: "My adversity lies in the land of Wu 吳, my time to avoid lies in the year of *you* 酉. But now I fear I cannot escape them."'
43 *Taiping guang ji* 81.520.
44 Wang Yun 王筠 (481–549) is known as a distinguished literary figure of emperor Wu's reign: he enjoyed a literary friendship with Shen Yue (note 20, above), and was one of the group of associates who assisted Xiao Tong in compiling the anthology *Wen xuan* (note 17, above): see *Liang shu* 33.485. The official appointment attached to him in this narrative, *Situ zuo zhangshi* 司徒左長史, was conferred in 530 (*ibid.* 33.486).
45 His topic is the location and procreative practice of the Land of Women in the far west: for a note on this see Glen Dudbridge,

The Hsi-yu chi: a study of antecedents to the sixteenth-century Chinese novel, Cambridge 1970, p. 13, n. 4.
46 Taiping guang ji 81.522.
47 Shi ji 74.2344.
48 Gu jin shuo hai 古今說海: 'Shuo yuan 說淵' 12, 'Zhenze long nü zhuan 震澤龍女傳'. The earliest known edition of this work has a preface dated 1544.
49 It can be added that parts of section A appear, under the title Liang si gong ji and attributed to Shen Yue of the Liang, in the late-Ming collection He ke san zhi 合刻三志 (printed edition in Naikaku Bunko). The item reproduces quite closely text from two episodes – the game of she fu and Wan Jie's account of foreign parts. It comes in a section headed 'Recording singularity' (zhi qi 志奇), and appears alongside accounts of remarkable Buddhists, Daoists, knights-errant, beauties, courtesans, etc. The same item, identical in text, pagination and lineation, reappears in the seventeenth-century expanded version of Shuo fu 說郛, but with two different features: the authorship is ascribed to Zhang Yue, and the text has been emended to omit the character yi 夷, 'barbarian', which was banned in the early Qing.
50 Donald McKenzie, Bibliography and the sociology of texts, p. 20.